Raisins & Almonds
... and Texas Oil!

Raisins & Almonds ...and Texas Oil!

JEWISH LIFE IN THE GREAT EAST TEXAS OIL FIELD

Jan Statman

SUNBELT EAKIN ★ Austin, Texas

P.O. Drawer 90159 ⬧ Austin, Texas 78709-0159
email: sales@eakinpress.com
⬚ website: www.eakinpress.com ⬚
1-57168-872-2
Library of Congress Control Number: 2004102628

For all the beautiful East Texans of every faith who have become such a loving part of my life, for my three East Texans, Charles Barry, Louis Craig, and Sherry Michelle, and most of all for Max, who brought me to this remarkable place.

With sincere appreciation to all the lovely people who shared their time, their photographs, and their stories to make this book a reality.

Contents

Introduction   ix

Chapter 1. Boomtown Days   1

Chapter 2. Dr. Ben Andres   13

Chapter 3. Ben Balter   19

Chapter 4. Ann and Norman (Notte) Balter   26

Chapter 5. Celia Bergman   41

Chapter 6. Phillip Brin   53

Chapter 7. Adele Daiches   59

Chapter 8. Al Davis   71

Chapter 9. Irving Falk   81

Chapter 10. Dan Felsenthal   88

Chapter 11. Milton Galoob, Sarah Picow,
            and Celia Bergman   91

Chapter 12. DeDe Gans   103

Chapter 13. Phil Hurwitz   111

Chapter 14. Louis Kariel Sr.   122

Chapter 15. Sam Krasner   126

Chapter 16. Hyman Laufer   128

Chapter 17. Yom Kippur   139

Chapter 18. "Mike" Marwil   140

Chapter 19. S. M. (Mendy) Rabicoff   148

Chapter 20. Vera Remer   160

Chapter 21. Joe and Carrie Riff   170

Chapter 22. Jay Sosland   172

Chapter 23. Nathan Waldman   179

Chapter 24. Sarah Richkie Whitehurst   193

Index   201

About the Author   209

Raisins and Almonds

Raisins and Almonds. The traditional Yiddish folk song whispered words of hope to a downtrodden people whose bitter lives offered few dreams and meager hope for the future. They were willing to leave home, family, friends, everything they knew, to make the perilous journey across the ocean to a strange new place where the only promise really offered was that somehow, by virtue of hard work and luck, they would be able to provide a better life for their children.

To people who were hungry much of the time, a treat of raisins and almonds represented a good life of unimaginable prosperity. The Jewish people who came to East Texas during the great oil boom worked hard to fulfil the promise of the good life. Theirs was a dream of raisins and almonds . . . and Texas oil!

Translated from the Yiddish by Jack Friedman, the words of the old song are sad but hopeful:

Raisins and Almonds
(*Rossentier un Mandlin*)

In the Great Sanctuary,
In a tiny corner,
Sits the young widow, alone.
She rocks her infant son, Yudele,
In his little cradle
And she sings him to sleep
With a sweet little lullaby:

"Under Yudele's cradle
Sits a pure white goat.
The goat will pull a small wagon
And carry goods to trade in the market.
Yudele, that will be your calling,
Raisins and almonds.
Sleep, my little one, sleep.
In time you will be a great merchant
And earn much money and happiness, my Yudele.
Sleep, my Yudele,
Sleep and dream
Of raisins and almonds.
Sleep, my little one, sleep."

Introduction

Jewish families lived in East Texas long before the oil boom. In 1850, Isaac Wolf came to Marshall from Syracuse, New York, went into the cotton brokerage business, and encouraged his nephews, Daniel and Mayer Doppelmayer, to join him there. Israel Levitt opened his tavern in Jefferson in 1854, one short year after the town was established. Jacob and Ernestine Sterne arrived in Jefferson in 1855. Although he had previously been one of the many Jewish peddlers traveling in the area, David Oppenheimer and his brother Anton established D&A Oppenheimer's in Rusk in 1858. Benjamin and Etta Brachfield left Vicksburg, Mississippi, to settle in Henderson in the 1870s.

Early Jewish families of East Texas often traveled to larger cities to celebrate religious holidays and special occasions, or they quietly practiced their religion within the sanctity of their homes as they worked to become vital members of their peaceful communities.

During the winter of 1930-31, while the Great Depression spread misery and hardship everywhere else in America, oil was discovered in East Texas, bringing a rush of prosperity to the quiet towns.

Jewish newcomers came in with the boom. They came from exotic locations, as distant as the shores of the Baltic Sea, and they came from every corner of America, from as far away as the coal mining towns of Pennsylvania, or as near as the oil-boom towns of Oklahoma. The newcomers arrived with resourcefulness fueled by desperation. They were willing to work as hard as the times.

The discovery of oil changed the landscape of the quiet East Texas towns and the countryside. Oil wells appeared among the pine and hardwood trees, springing up in forests and in pastures.
—Photo courtesy Max Statman

The best way to understand the people and to experience the true flavor of those boomtown days is to learn of their experiences in their own words, as they lived them. They are presented here as a series of brief biographies. Some will tell about faraway adventures. Others will tell about working on the railroads, or in the steel mills, or in the oil patch. Some will tell how Grandfather dined with Indians in the Oklahoma Territory, or how Grandmother watched the first discovery well come in shaking the earth with a terrible force until black oil spewed across the derrick's top. Since they were the true observers, some will tell a story one way, and others will tell the same story quite differently.

There are tales of hardship and tales of romance, even stories of good times during those hard times. Each of these men and women takes us back a time when the constant noise of drilling rigs pounded the ears and stirred the heart, when oilfield pipe drilled deep into the earth and when black oil spewed high above the poor-boy wells, when gas flares lit the oilfield nights and Hebrew prayers were recited in the room above the fire station. They open the screen door so you can peek into the past to meet the people who were willing to pick up stakes and put down roots in a wild and woolly boom town.

As Americans, as Texans, and as Jews, they brought their unique perspective to East Texas. They contributed to the growing success of their communities.

CHAPTER 1

Boomtown Days

When three discovery wells opened the vast East Texas Oilfield in the winter of 1930 and spring of 1931, the Piney Woods bloomed with the black treasure that would change East Texas forever. It was oil, black gold.

The drought of 1929 had ruined the cotton crop. King Cotton's fall undermined the stability of banks in the Gregg County seat of Longview. Still reeling from cotton and banking failures, that city saw the Texas and Pacific Railroad move its terminal to Mineola, taking its employees, its payroll, and the city's prosperity with it. Businesses failed. Homes and farms were lost. And then the Great Depression hit.

Desperate people, eagerly searching for a ray of hope, focused on the dream of oil. Oil had been discovered in Ranger, Cisco, Breckenridge, Burkburnett, El Dorado, Amarillo, and many other towns—why not in East Texas? But that slim hope was dashed when petroleum engineers and geologists of the nation's major oil companies declared there was absolutely no oil whatsoever anywhere in the area.

In spite of those declarations, legendary wildcatter C. M. "Dad" Joiner succeeded in finding oil on Sunday, October 5, 1930, when his discovery well, the Daisy Bradford No. 3, blew in a gusher at Turnertown, near Henderson in Rusk County, producing at an unbelievable rate.

"Everybody in town broke their necks to get out there to see the

The discovery of oil changed the face of the peaceful East Texas communities.
—Photo by Max Statman

Completion of the Daisy Bradford No. 3, October 5, 1929. This famous photograph shows Dad Joiner congratulating Doc Lloyd as H. L. Hunt, Ed C. Laster, and crew members look on.

—Photo in the collection of Jan Statman

well come in," "Mike" Marwil described the scene. "First you felt the earth tremble and shake, then you saw black oil shooting as high as the derrick. People were beside themselves! They wallowed in the oil! Just swam in it! They rubbed it all over themselves. They had to be told to put out their cigarettes for fear they would blow us all up."

Two months later, on Christmas Day, 1930, Ed Bateman's Lou Della Crim No. 3 came in on the Crim Farm outside Kilgore in Gregg County, producing three times the volume of the Daisy Bradford No. 3. The Lou Della Crim well was followed on January 26, 1930, by the equally lucrative F. K. Lathrop No. 1, eleven miles to the north and east in Pine Tree, near Longview, also in Gregg County. The three successful discovery wells outlined the boundaries of the great East Texas Oilfield. The "Black Giant" was forty-two miles long and eight miles wide. The sound of the "boom" was heard around the world.

Engineers and geologists of the major oil companies realized they had made a major mistake. The sudden oil prosperity prompted Longview's Judge Erskine Bramlette to declare, "At last, the waters have opened up to let the Children of Israel out of the land of bondage. The boom is here, and it looks good."

Judge Bramlette did not realize how prophetic his words would be. As America reeled under the shock of the global depression, many Jewish people were among those who found their way to the sleepy towns of East Texas. They came seeking hope in a nation where there was no hope, jobs in a nation where there was no work, opportunity in a nation where there were only "hard times when you're down and out."

"We all came C.O.D.," Celia Bergman explained. "That's cash-on-delivery. We didn't have any money, but we had youth and strength. We were determined to survive the depression. And we made it!"

Some went to work in the oilfield itself. Some went into services supplying the oilfields, trading scrap metal, pipe, oil well equipment, and supplies. Some opened pipe yards and scrap yards. Others opened small shops to provide necessities that made the lives of oil-field workers and their families bearable.

Some became actively involved in the business of oil. Joe Gerson managed and was engineer of H. L. Hunt's Parade Refining Company near Turnertown. At a time when oilfield workers worked

Tyler Street, downtown Longview, Texas, before the wells came in.

—Courtesy the Gregg County Historical Foundation

around the clock, seven days a week, the Travis and Livingston families, Orthodox Jews, shut their cable tool drilling rigs down from Friday evening to Saturday evening in observance of the Sabbath, allowing their workers a day of rest.

Others worked day and night, forcing their small businesses to succeed by the remarkable effort of their will.

Celia and Dave Bergman arrived in Longview at night. "The mud was eighteen inches deep, and the lights of the drilling rigs were just a-going like fire," Celia said. "They were diamonds in the sky! I was brought up in the oilfield towns of Oklahoma, so this looked like home to me. I loved it, and we stayed."

Those who could put a few coins together wanted to "get into the action," to buy into a well that would make their dreams come true. Sometimes they did. More often, they did not. Marshall merchant Louis Kariel was involved in a number of leases which, he said, "helped define the edge of the field."

The old red brick Gregg County Courthouse was overrun by oilmen, wildcatters, speculators, and lease hounds. The county clerk was suddenly the busiest man in town. It became necessary for him to form "reading groups" to work in shifts around the clock, researching land titles stored in old record books streaked with dust, faded by time, and stuffed into the cobwebbed corners of the old courthouse.

Tent cities grew up overnight. Kilgore swelled from a farming community of 500 to a crowded boom town of more than 10,000. Sam Krasner and his brother Barney rode into Kilgore on a truckload of seven-inch pipe. "Kilgore was a booming shack town," he said. "Although some of the town's original buildings could still be seen, most of the buildings were hastily constructed of tin, or sheet iron."

Wells grew up in rose gardens and in door yards. Oil was discovered beneath a bank in downtown Kilgore. A twenty-four-foot section was sliced off the rear of six downtown businesses, and six wells were sunk into the ground with the legs of their derricks touching. They formed the richest half-acre in the world.

There wasn't enough food to feed the hungry "boomers." There wasn't enough room to house them. Strangers slept in chicken coops, on parlor floors, in attic lofts, and outdoors under the open sky.

"When I came home from college that spring, I still had my bedroom," Sarah Richkie Whitehurst said. "Many of my friends could not say as much. People rented rooms and parts of rooms. Some even rented cot space on the parlor floor. Some rented beds for so many hours and when that time was up, someone else came in to sleep."

Those who could find no shelter slept on the courthouse lawn. Joe Riff was fortunate enough to rent a room located diagonally across the Courthouse Square from his store. He said, "Every morning when I walked across the courthouse lawn to go to work, I was obliged to step over the reclining bodies of men and women who were sleeping out in the weather, covering themselves as best they could with old newspapers and shreds of blankets."

Derricks popped up like mushrooms after a spring rain. And the rain came down in torrents! It rained forty days and forty nights. Worn by the rains and the weight of heavy oil field machinery, the meager country roads turned into narrow ribbons of mud. Old settlers sat on their fretwork front porches and watched their way of life change before their eyes. Some kept their distance from the noisy goings-on, and some became wealthy in spite of themselves.

Working as a "lease hound" or land man, Ben Balter attempted to buy the mineral rights to a small farm, but the farmer's widow insisted that he buy the entire farm. "All I want to do is to get away from this crazy place," she told him. And she did.

The growing need for oilfield law attracted young attorneys. Phillip Brin's first paycheck was $15 for a week's work. "In those depression days, you were so happy to have a job you didn't demand to know what you were going to be paid," he explained, "It didn't cost much to live if you could manage to come by the few pennies. We saw many a starving person riding on the railroad boxcars as they came through town."

Doctors were needed. Pediatrician Ben Andres said, "The practice of medicine was a much more personal thing in that day and time. You knew your patients' families, you knew what they did and who they were."

Smiley Rabicoff made a lot of money manufacturing and selling whiskey during Prohibition, but he was out of business when Prohibition was repealed. His father-in-law, Harry Sobol, told him, "There's a good opportunity to make a living down here in the Texas oilfield. You buy something. You find somebody to buy it from you. You sell it and you make the difference."

Eighteen-year-old Adele Daiches was dismayed by her first sight of Kilgore. "When I got off that train at the Kilgore Depot, I found the streets were filled with mud. I later learned it was dust when it was not mud. You had a choice that spring, dust or mud."

Seventeen-year-old Milton Galoob drove his old Ford truck from Oklahoma to Longview on two tires and two rims. "I was out of work and hungry. I didn't have money for tires, but I knew that if I could manage to get here, my sister, Celia Bergman, would find a way to feed me."

Another eighteen-year-old, Irving Falk, came to the oilfield straight from his family's New Jersey dairy farm. "I didn't know whether to look up, look down, look sideways, or to just look out for traffic," he said. "Kilgore was a dense forest of oil derricks. There were approximately one thousand oil wells being drilled. There were twenty-five or thirty thousand oil wells in the field. Kilgore alone had a thousand wells. Some wells were producing as much as five thousand barrels a day. Back home in New Jersey, people weren't able to feed their children, but here in East Texas they were dressed up with gold belt buckles and fancy cowboy boots with silver tips that cost $150. That was a fortune in those days."

Oilfield workers didn't trust their money to banks, but they trusted the honest Jewish merchants. On payday, the merchants would cash the oilfield workers' checks. This meant the merchants would keep a lot of cash on hand on payday, and the crooks knew exactly when payday rolled around.

Nathan Waldman's parents, Joe and Clara Waldman, were robbed at gunpoint. "The robbers marched my parents to the back of the store and told them to sit down," he said. "My mother's diamond wedding ring was exposed, and Dad kept trying to call her attention to it, trying to warn her to turn the ring around or try to hide it. His frantic warnings became so obvious that the robbers finally said, "Don't worry, mister. We wouldn't take the lady's wedding ring away from her. All we want is your money!"

Thieves, prostitutes, and gamblers swarmed into the towns. Decent citizens were outraged. Help was summoned, and help arrived. One quiet afternoon, four shabbily dressed strangers stepped from a train outside Kilgore. They drew little attention. Scruffy-looking strangers were hardly uncommon in the oilfield. There was something different about these men, though. It was in their proud bearing and clear eyes. Legendary Texas Rangers had come upon the scene.

On a sunny day in early March, the leader of the group, Texas Ranger Sgt. Manuel T. "Lone Wolf" Gonzaullas, shed his drifter's disguise. He mounted his spirited black stallion for his famed ride down Kilgore's Main Street. His tanned face was clean-shaven; his boots and spurs gleamed in the morning light. An automatic rifle rested in his saddle holster. His pearl-handled six-shooters were ready at his hip.

The cry went up, "It's 'Lone Wolf' Gonzaullas! He's hard, but he's fair!"

Gonzaullas declared martial law and gave the criminals twenty-four hours to get out of town. Many abandoned their belongings in their rush to leave. The Texas Rangers began a series of lightning raids. Three hundred arrests were made that day.

Kilgore had never needed a jail, so there was no proper place to hold the prisoners. Lone Wolf had trace chains and padlocks secured to a heavy length of chain and run the full length of the Baptist church. When his prisoners were tethered to it, it was promptly labeled "Lone Wolf's Trot Line."

Lone Wolf often determined a man's guilt or innocence simply by looking at his hands. Oilfield workers had rough, work-worn hands. Crooks and gamblers had soft hands with manicured fingernails. Lone Wolf's soft-hand test did not bode well for Hyman Hurwitz, a soft-handed young haberdasher who worked late one night after curfew. "Hyman thought the Rangers wouldn't bother him," his brother, Phillip Hurwitz, explained. "No sooner did he step through the door of his shop than Lone Wolf picked him up. The Ranger handcuffed Hyman to the trot line, and he remained there until other Jewish merchants came to rescue him."

Hyman Laufer joined the National Guard as a college student during the summer of 1931 and was sent to Gladewater, where law and order had completely broken down.

"Every thief, every thug, every lawbreaker had found his way into East Texas," Laufer said. "More than that, there was a flood of oil coming out of this field. The governor declared the oilfield off-limits and shut the free production down. Many oilmen resented this and began running 'hot oil,' that is, illegal oil. The National Guard was expected to patrol the oilfield, but we were often misled.

"We would go up to a well and we would see that the valve on the well was operating, so we would turn it off, or we thought we had.

Oilmen installed valves that worked in reverse. We would actually be turning it on! There were many other such subterfuges and clever devices to keep the hot oil running."

The discovery of oil meant a return to former prosperity for some East Texans. Vera Remer's family, the Brachfields, had lived in Henderson since 1874. Her uncle, Charles Brachfield, was a distinguished Rusk County judge and state senator. Her father, Mose Marwil, was mayor of Henderson.

"During the boom, the streets were filled with people, but they weren't the sort of people you would want to associate with," she said. "Old-timers considered oilfield workers to be roughnecks and riff-raff."

To others it meant a swift ride to unheard-of wealth. East Texas towns saw more than an adequate supply of ostentation. Schoolgirls appeared in classrooms dressed in ball gowns and tiaras. Diamond rings sold like crackerjacks. Before long, well-known Dallas retail establishments such as Neiman-Marcus and the A. Harris Co. were dressing the beautiful women of East Texas in the latest fashions.

Ladies took the Southern Pacific train to Dallas, ate breakfast on the train, shopped, dined in the luxurious dining car, and were home before 8:40 in the evening.

"People wanted to dress well," DeDe Gans explained. "Neiman's was a front runner of fashion, and having Neiman's nearby set the pace for us. A group of us would go into Dallas to shop and have lunch, and we would really make a day of it."

"A lot of people will tell you that the oil boom was exciting," Celia Bergman remembered. "But for us the exciting part was that we'd open the store at nine o'clock in the morning and we wouldn't leave until ten o'clock at night."

"We opened the store at 6:30 in the morning," Phil Hurwitz agreed. "Drillers and roughnecks would be going to work at that hour. We'd close the store at nine, ten, eleven o'clock, whenever the last man was off the street. Then we'd go to Mattie's Ballroom and dance all night, take a shower, lie down for an hour, get up, and go back to work at 6:30 in the morning. It was an exciting experience for a sixteen-year-old boy!"

The new East Texans were determined to maintain their Jewish identity in the oilpatch. "At first they met at the different stores," Nathan Waldman explained. "They held Sunday school for the children at Sam Goldman's store, or at Smiley Rabicoff's store. Much of the time it was so hot that they would open the doors, but because of the Blue Laws, the police would make them shut the doors again. Sunday school became really hot stuff."

Reform Jews attended High Holy Day Services at Temple Moses Montifiore in Marshall. Orthodox and Conservative Jews held informal High Holy Day Services in the hall above McCarley's Jewelry store in Longview or above the fire station in Kilgore. Services were interrupted when the fire alarm sounded, and it sounded often in the oilfield town. The congregation would rush to the windows to see what was on fire and if their help was needed.

The women of Kilgore convinced the men they needed a synagogue. The men said, "Fine, you raise a thousand dollars and we'll raise the rest."

The women took up the challenge. They held a "well baby" contest to determine who was the healthiest baby in town. Doctors examined the babies and selected the winners. Children of many oilfield workers received health check-ups they otherwise would have lacked. The women raised their share, and the men came through with their part of the bargain.

Kilgore's Beth Sholom Synagogue was organized in 1936. "It was not a very big building," Mendy Rabicoff remembered. "When the congregation outgrew the little building, Hyman Hurwitz located an old wood frame honkeytonk, which was moved to the location and 'reformed' to serve as the community's social hall."

The young congregation had some interesting rabbis, including the poker playing rabbi, the rabbi with the eccentric wife, and the rabbi who was chased by the horse.

"There was a pasture behind the synagogue," Nathan Waldman said. "Our Christian neighbor kept his horse pastured there. The rabbi was dreadfully afraid of the horse, and the horse was not too fond of the rabbi, either. One Friday evening, the rabbi decided to take a shortcut across the pasture. The horse took offense and ran toward the rabbi. The rabbi ran toward the synagogue. The horse ran faster. The rabbi ran even faster, proving that when properly motivated, an Orthodox rabbi can outrun a Christian horse!"

Hyman Laufer said, "We had members from Kilgore, Longview, Henderson, Gladewater, Overton, and other towns. We clung together like ducks on a pond. We had Sunday school picnics and barbecues, dances and parties. We had a lot of fun and a lot of love. After all, this was our home."

Three discovery wells transformed the region's economy. An economic map of the time described the economically troubled nation with white marks for depressed areas and gray for less troubled areas, but East Texas was inked with solid black. It was the black gold of prosperity.

The Jewish community gathered from many exotic corners of the world, only to find themselves in the most exotic place of all. East Texas in the boom!

CHAPTER 2

Dr. Ben Andres

"At that time the practice of medicine was a much more personal thing. They could call me at any hour of the day or night and talk to me when they needed me."

The wildest days of the oil boom were over by the time my wife Bea and I arrived in Longview on April 1, 1936, but there was still plenty of excitement to go around.

I was graduated from medical school in 1932 and had a year's internship at Parkland Hospital in Dallas. Bea and I both grew up in Dallas, and we had known each other since we were teenagers. We were married in Dallas after I completed my internship.

We went to New York where I completed my residency. I had to find a way to earn enough money to open my practice, so I joined the old Civilian Conservation Corps, the CCC. They were paying $263 a month, which doesn't sound like much now, although it was a considerable amount of money at that time.

We spent six weeks at Fort Dix in New Jersey, and then they sent me to Sacramento, California. We spent thirty-six hours on the bus because the bus was the cheapest way to go from New York to Chicago. Then we spent three days sitting up on the train from Chicago to Sacramento! We were young and we were able to do things like that without any permanent ill effects.

The regional office in Sacramento sent me to a camp in Murphy's, California, which is in the gold field country. I was the medical officer, and I had three auxiliary camps to visit. We were up in the mountains, at about 2,300 feet, although some of the camps I had to visit were up as high as 5,000 feet.

There were about two hundred New York City slum boys between the ages of eighteen and twenty living at the camp. During the depression, the CCC sent boys from the eastern cities to California to build roads through the foothills of the Sierras. With all those slum kids running around, we could still wander the trails in the woods alone at any hour of the day or night without being concerned for our safety. Think of that in modern times! These were decent, honest young men who were proud to be able to work, and they built great things for our country.

We stayed with the CCC for six months. Then we came back to Texas, hoping to find a place that needed a pediatrician. We landed in Longview quite accidentally. A detail man phoned and told me to take a look at Henderson. Now, you must understand that a detail man is the representative of the pharmaceutical company who calls on physicians to demonstrate his company's new products and drugs. Without the detail man, it would be impossible for doctors to keep up with the newest drugs and products on the market. Because of his mobility, the detail man is in a position to know what is happening throughout the medical community.

Bea and I went to Henderson, but we could see it wasn't going to work out, so we drove to Longview to spend the night. We saw the name "Riff" on a store downtown and remembered that Carrie Riff of Longview was the aunt of Sam Scher, with whom I had graduated from medical school. We stopped into the store and talked to the Riffs. They encouraged us to talk to the doctors in Longview. The town had twelve thousand people and only thirteen doctors. All of them were general practitioners, except Dr. Hurst, who had an ear-nose-and-throat clinic. There was no pediatrician. It sounded good, and we decided to stay. We rented an office in the Glover-Crim building downtown for $40 a month. We rented half a duplex for $40 a month, and we figured that if we could gross $200 a month we would break even. My wife worked as my office nurse until our children, David and Joyce came along. Fortunately, pediatricians didn't require much equipment to get started in those days. The office had a little waiting room and an examining room with my desk and the pediatric table. We started each day by waiting for patients.

At first, people weren't sure about what I was doing. Some of them mistook the pediatrician for a podiatrist, but I was patient in explaining my specialty so that the confusion was soon straightened out. The practice grew rapidly because people liked the idea of having specialized care for their children.

At that time the practice of medicine was a much more personal thing. Sometimes, when I went out on a house call, I had to crawl up into the bed to examine the older children. I knew my patients' families. I was in their houses. I was involved with them and their children, I genuinely cared about them as human beings, and we became personal friends.

They could call me at any hour of the day or night and talk to me when they needed me. Of course I would never think of charging a patient for phone calls. I learned to answer the phone half a dozen times during the night, go back to sleep immediately, and in the morning I would remember to write down everybody's conversations and what I had told them to do. Anxious mothers could call a dozen times during the night. The children probably got along just as well as they do now, but it was much more reassuring for the mothers.

House calls were a definite part of routine pediatric care. I was in the office during the day, but I would often find it necessary to leave the office to go to a patient's home and see about a sick child. When my practice was so busy that I was seeing fifty or sixty patients a day, I had to route my house calls in the evening before I went home. Caring for children is something you cannot "turn off" at the end of the day, no matter how long the day might have been. Many times, I would wake up in the middle of the night thinking about a sick child in the hospital. I would get dressed and go back to see how he was doing. I was often at the hospital day and night.

I recently met a man in his forties who said, "You don't remember me, but I was in an accident when I was two years old. I was hospitalized at the old Markham Hospital for about six weeks and you took care of me."

I've had so many patients over the years that I honestly did not remember him. He was not satisfied with that, so the following week he brought his mother by to give me the whole story.

She said, "You took care of my son from the time he was born. He was unconscious for a week after the accident and you sat up with him day and night."

That made such an impression on those people that they were eager to come back and say hello to me after forty-five years had passed!

I couldn't practice these days, because medicine has become too impersonal and too mechanized, to say nothing of the insurance forms and malpractice suits that doctors are burdened with. When we opened our clinic here, all of our insurance for everything for all three doctors as well as the building was $125 a year. You never heard of a malpractice case that was not justified. I think the personal contact between the physician and his patients made a big difference. The families you cared for knew that you were doing the best you could for them, and they appreciated it.

There were no antibiotics, so that the mortality rate for acute diseases was higher. One year we had a very nasty streptococci pneumonia epidemic and we lost three children. It was tragic. We had a polio epidemic and we suffered a couple of deaths. There was no polio vaccine to prevent it. There was only supportive treatment. That applied to almost everything we did. I never saw a case of Sudden Infant Death Syndrome, which we now hear so much about, but doctors still have the same problems with colic that I had. I don't think they've solved that problem, even after fifty years.

We took care of newborns in much the same way they take care of newborns now, but doctors now seem to be seeing more newborns with various types of problems. That may be because of the sheer number of babies.

The first year I was here I had two very tiny prematures. They weighed a little over two pounds each. Such things are almost routine now, but at that time such survival was almost unheard of. Fortunately, my first two tiny prematures survived. And they had no eye problems, because we did not have the high-powered incubators with the high concentration of oxygen that can cause blindness in tiny prematures. All we had to give them was oxygen by mask. We watched them, and when they turned blue, we gave them oxygen. That was it. It may sound primitive now, but that was all we could do for them.

That was before doctors realized that the high concentration of oxygen was causing eye problems in very small prematures. I spoke with several New York doctors, trying to find out what I did or did not do that was different from what they did or did not do. I wanted to know why I did not see this problem in Longview, Texas, and they saw so much of it in New York City. A close friend was an associate professor of pediatrics at Cornell Medical Center in New York City. We discussed it, and we may have had the answer years before the Presbyterian Hospital in New York finally realized that the high concentration of oxygen caused the problem. At that time, the belief was that oxygen was good for you, and the more the better!

It wasn't until 1948 or '49 that we learned about newborns with severe jaundice (for which we did exchange transfusions) when they had an RH negative mother and and RH positive infant. We did the first exchange transfusion in East Texas in 1949. The first baby I did an exchange on happened to be the child of a Jewish family living in Kilgore. These people have remained close friends, and the boy is now a stockbroker with Merrill Lynch. They have elaborate machinery to perform this procedure now, but we only had a little piece of rubber tubing. Another pediatrician and I did the exchange with multiple syringes.

Dr. Cook and Dr. Rushing were both general practitioners with large practices. They wanted to build a clinic. They asked me to be the third partner, and we built a building in 1939. I was the only Jewish doctor in town, and they did not hesitate to ask me to join them. I had a small practice compared with theirs, but they offered me a partnership. My patients never cared what my religion might be. All they cared about was that I would help cure their sick children.

Our neighbors here in East Texas have always been decent people. Since East Texas is deep in the Bible Belt, you might have expected to find anti-Semitism here, yet we ran into no feelings of that type. The Jewish people of Longview have always contributed to our community, and we have always been welcomed as an important part of the community.

During World War II, the County Medical Society decided that all the eligible doctors in the county should volunteer for service. Almost all of them were accepted, and it pretty nearly cleaned out our medical population. We had such a serious shortage of doctors in East Texas that those of us who remained had to work that much harder to care for all the patients. I also volunteered, but I was rejected.

We attended synagogue in Kilgore, and much of our Jewish life involved our small community. We visited each other's homes, had our weekly poker games and our weekly dinners. We were members of the Pinecrest Country Club. Later, after we built our Temple in Longview, Rabbi Harvey Wessel came here from Tyler to teach our children. He was a splendid, elegant, well-educated man. Our son and daughter were confirmed here in Longview.

My parents came to this country from Russia in 1907. They both grew up in a little town called Pydosia near the naval base at Sevastapol on the Crimean Peninsula. My father, Isaac Andres, spent eighteen months in a Czarist prison because of his Revolutionary activities. The next time the officials caught him they said, "You will either get out of the country or you will take a one-way trip to Siberia." So he left Russia.

Many Eastern European Jewish immigrants came to this country steerage. They came to America with nothing but the will to work unbelievably hard to earn a living. Although the majority of immigrants landed at Ellis Island and remained in New York City, my father's ship came in at Galveston, so he settled in Texas. My mother, Anna Slayfield Andres, joined him a year later and they were married in Waco. From there, they moved to Dallas, where I was born in 1910.

My wife Bea's parents came from Rumania to Dallas when Bea was only a year old. When we came to Longview, we were living the American dream as our parents had dreamed it.

CHAPTER 3

Ben Balter

Gathered from various sources:

Ben Balter was widely acknowledged to be the Longview Jewish community's Renaissance man. Although he was a successful oil-man, he was an avid reader of the classics as well as of contemporary literature. He was an accomplished musician—a violinist and com-poser who provided a host of original music scores and arrangements which were used by the organists of Temple Emanu-El of Longview.

He was an art collector, businessman, fisherman, farmer, Torah scholar, and teacher. He was justifiably proud of the facility with which he could read from, translate, and interpret the Torah and its commentaries. He taught many of the young boys of the congrega-tion to read Hebrew and prepared a great many of them to become Bar Mitzvah.

When he was a young man in Pennsylvania, Ben studied to be-come a Rabbi but abandoned that pursuit in favor of studying for the law. The depression interrupted his education and caused him to move to Texas in search of employment. As an interesting expla-nation of the life and times in which he lived, Ben always said his father strongly believed that every boy should learn a trade in addi-tion to whatever career he might choose. Ben's father was a butcher, and Ben was obliged to train as a butcher before he could hope to study law.

His cousin Sid Balter played football for Centenary College in

Ben Balter

—Photo courtesy of Ada Milstein

Shreveport and became friendly with many of the young Jewish peo-
ple in that city. Sid's sister Minnie came to visit him in Shreveport.
While visiting, she became friendly with a pretty young girl named
Marguerite Maritsky. Minnie invited Marguerite to visit her in
Pennsylvania, where she met Ben.

Ben described Marguerite by saying, "She was the prettiest creature I had ever seen in my entire life. She was pretty, she was smart, and she was talented. I was determined to marry her."

They were married in Shreveport.

A short time after their daughter Harriet was born, Ben became ill with a debilitating ailment that left him bedridden for many months. After a long recuperation, he was only able to walk with the help of crutches. Marguerite's uncle, Izzy Maritsky, owned a men's clothing store in Longview and suggested that the young couple move nearby.

"I arrived in Longview on crutches, with a wife and child to support," Ben said, "I was told that I could find work if I would go see a certain man and do whatever that man told me to do without asking too many nosey questions."

The man gave the young stranger on crutches a handful of thousand-dollar bills and said, "Go see Mr. X and tell him you want to buy a tank from him."

"I was desperate. I did as I was told and I didn't ask too many nosey questions," Ben admitted, "I was soon hobbling between one oilman and another, my pockets loaded with thousand-dollar bills, carrying out the business of buying and selling tanks. I never asked what was in the tanks. I assumed they were empty, but I later learned they were full of oil. I thought I was buying and selling empty tanks, but I was buying and selling hot oil. I knew nothing about the oil they contained!"

Ben soon became aware of illegal goings-on in the oilfield towns. An acquaintance worked for an oil refinery in Gladewater. The refinery was legally permitted to process a specific number of gallons of oil each day. The oil came in through their pipeline and was carefully measured by government agents. By an interesting coincidence, the city's storm sewer system ended only a few feet from a refinery. Before long, hot oil was flowing into the refinery through the city's storm sewers and was secretly processed at night, virtually under the noses of government agents.

Another acquaintance noticed that at a certain point in the oilfield, the pipeline for refinery A and the pipeline for refinery B were only a few feet apart. Refinery A ran its legal oil in the mornings while refinery B ran its legal oil in the afternoons. Ben's enterprising young acquaintance bought used oilfield pipe and stealthily made a crossover connection. He then went to refinery A and said, "I can get you all the oil you want, running wide open, but you can only get it in the afternoons and you mustn't ask where it came from." Refinery A was delighted to pay him for his oil. He went to refinery B with the same story. He could get all the oil they could use, but he could only provide it in the mornings and they mustn't ask questions. Refinery B was also delighted with the opportunity to buy all the oil he could provide. By switching valves, the young man ran oil from refinery B into refinery A's pipeline all afternoon, and he ran oil from refinery A into refinery B's pipeline all morning. Of course it was theft, but Ben was quick to point out that his young acquaintance was not greedy. He ran the "crossover" only long enough to get his grubstake. Then he dug it up and went home to West Texas, where he used the money to build a million-dollar business.

Ben was gradually able to recover from his illness. "I thought it was probably a good idea to distance myself from the hot oil business," he explained.

He took a job working for Sklar and Dorfman, who were legitimate oil operators. They hired him to work at $25 a week. Since he had extensive training in law school, they could ask him all the legal questions he could answer, but since he had not completed law school, they didn't have to pay legal fees! At that time he was happy to have the job.

"After that, I decided to use what I knew of the butcher business to operate the Pig Trail Inn, a small restaurant in downtown Longview."

He later became a "land man," an oil company representative who leases land for potential well sites. He was leasing oil rights on farmland in the area when he met an old woman who offered him an unusual proposal. She was not interested in selling the oil rights to her property, but she was willing to sell the whole farm, land and oil rights together, for the same money. Ben was astonished by this offer. He did not want to take advantage of her, so he suggested she think about it more carefully.

She told him she was a widow who always hated living on that farm. By buying the land, he would finally set her free. He would be doing her the biggest favor of her life! Always the gentleman, he could not resist the opportunity to do a good deed for the lady. He bought the property, leased the land, and leased the oil rights.

Although he was not a farmer, Ben learned an interesting lesson as a result of finding a different piece of farmland. "While working as a land man I came upon an underdeveloped farm that was blessed with a well located on top of a hill. It could provide water for irrigation, and with certain judicious farming methods the farm could be restored to productivity. I offered the farmer the opportunity to be my partner. I would provide the capital. He would provide the labor, and we would share the profits equally."

Ben was certain the East Texas land, which had been ruined by the overplanting of cotton, could be encouraged to support other valuable crops. He sent a soil sample to his brother, an agricultural scientist back in Pennsylvania, and asked what crops would be appropriate to the land and to the climate. The answer returned: "Grow peanuts and grapes." East Texas could become prime grape country, eventually even supporting a first-rate wine industry!

While Ben made plans to build and promote this newfound industry, he realized that the local grocery stores were obliged to purchase fresh vegetables from distant places so that they seldom arrived on East Texas tables in prime condition. He remembered the successful truck farms of the Northeast. Surely, his farm could produce fresh vegetables, and provide them earlier in the season than distant produce that was hauled into the area.

"I discussed the possibilities with area grocery store owners and they promised to buy as much fresh produce as I could provide, even if it was necessary to pay premium prices. So I decided to plant vegetables on the farm while preparing the land for grapes."

He offered the farmer a chance at participating in this opportunity. Ben would provide money for seed, fertilizer, and other necessary materials, while the farmer would provide the labor and expertise. The ramshackle farm was soon transformed into a productive haven of beautiful, abundant produce.

Their first crop was outstanding. True to their word, area grocers bought every bit of the fresh produce at premium prices, happy to be able to make it available to their customers. The farm made a tidy profit, which Ben immediately shared with his partner.

Much to his surprise, his farmer-partner pleaded with Ben to withhold his share of the profits. This was unthinkable! The farmer had worked hard, and he was entitled to be paid. Ben insisted in turning over a large sum of money, along with seed and fertilizer for future crops.

When Ben visited the farm several weeks later, he found it had returned to its earlier unfortunate state. Fences were not mended. The land had not been tilled, and weeds grew in fields where seeds had never been planted. Hungry dogs barked at the corners of the house and the screen door hung on a broken hinge. Ben found his partner inside the filthy house, hopelessly drunk and lying on the unmade bed amid a pile of broken bottles.

"I begged you not to give me all that money!" The man chided him. "You did this to me! This is all your fault."

Never having seen such a large amount of money, the man could not handle the inevitable stress it brought into his life and was ruined by his success.

The partnership was dissolved.

When Ben's father came from Pennsylvania to East Texas to visit his family, Ben and Marguerite's many Longview and Kilgore friends entertained him lavishly and hospitably. Wishing to reciprocate their hospitality, Ben and Marguerite planned to host a large dinner party. Ben's father insisted on selecting the meat. Father and son went to the Norton and Barbee grocery store in downtown Longview to purchase a large quantity of beef.

Back in Pennsylvania, the Balters were well known as a family of skilled butchers. Ben's father selected a particularly handsome side of beef, but when the local butcher began to slice the meat, it was obvious that his work was inferior. He was cutting against the grain and making poor cuts. Unfortunately, Ben's father was a man of limited patience. Old as he was, he leaped across the counter, seized the cleaver, and began to chase the incompetent meat cutter around the store!

He was finally restrained. and while the local butcher cowered, Ben's father proceeded to carve the meat himself, explaining how and why he was making certain cuts, forming the beef into acceptable and appropriate sections. He was not satisfied until the man had learned something of his trade.

Ben always retained his fascination with the world and his youthful enthusiasm for all that was in it. In his later years he said, "I am the same person I have always been. I just feel like a young boy looking out through an old window."

Ben and Marguerite's daughter Harriet married Harry Mellon of Houston. Harriet and Harry had three children, Rebecca, Mark, and Stephen Mellon.

When they both retired, Ben and his friend Dave Bergman became "fishing buddies." They made a science of fishing. It became their dedicated hobby. Ben would frequently host fish fries for his friends.

Ben was active in planning the new building for Longview's Temple Emanu-El. Speaking at the dedication of the Temple on November 16, 1958, Ben said, "We dedicate this Temple and ourselves to the service of God and to this community. We always remember how 'pleasant it is for brothers to dwell together in unity.'"

CHAPTER 4

Ann and Norman (Notte) Balter

"You're the first Jew we've ever seen who would work this hard. There's never been a Jew who would work in the steel mill before."

East Texas may sound like a strange place for two kids from Freedom, Pennsylvania, to pick for a honeymoon, but that's what Ann and I did. Times were hard during the depression, and people back home in Pennsylvania couldn't afford fancy trips. We got married and we came here to visit my cousin Ben Balter and his wife, Marguerite. Ben owned the Pig Trail Inn and worked for Sam Dorfman, who owned the Dorfman Oil Company.

I wasn't new to East Texas. I had been to this part of the country before. In fact, my sister Minnie and all our brothers had been here, too. My brother Sidney had been recruited to play football for Centenary College in Shreveport. Sidney was one hell of a football player. The Centenary coach, Jap Dowd, came to Pennsylvania to recruit a bunch of big, tough steelworkers and coal mining boys. The four boys Jap Dowd recruited all played football together at Freedom High School.

When Sid went to Centenary, he knew he was going to an "outlaw" team, and that was part of the attraction. Although they didn't belong to any conference at that time, Centenary beat Texas A&M, the University of Texas, and every other team in the Southwest

Conference. The oilman Archie Hanes furnished the money they needed to build themselves into a football powerhouse. Sid made all-American while he played for Centenary.

It shouldn't surprise anybody to hear that the boys were paid to play in those days, and they were paid good money, too. Football was probably more honest and above-board back then. Jap Dowd couldn't have hoped to shake those tough boys out of the steel mills and the coal mines with nothing more than a promise of rah-rah school spirit and good wishes. They were in it for the money, pure and simple.

Shreveport turned out to be a romantic place for our family. My brother Sid met his wife, Ray, there. She was a Shreveport girl. My cousin Ben met his wife, Marguerite, when she came from Shreveport to Pennsylvania to visit my sister Minnie. Ben started going down south to court her. Of course he said he was just coming south to look for business opportunities, but he didn't fool us for a minute. We all knew what he was up to.

Marguerite's uncle, Izzy Maritsky, owned a men's clothing store in Longview. About a year after Marguerite and Ben married, they moved to Longview. Ben was sick, their daughter Harriet was only a baby, and Izzy said there were opportunities here. Ben eventually went to work for Sam Dorfman. My cousin Ben was a smart fellow. He studied law. At one time he even studied to become a rabbi. He was a Torah scholar in addition to his other scholarship. He was talented, too. He played the violin with the Philadelphia Symphony Orchestra.

Marguerite introduced my sister Minnie to Milton Galoob when Minnie came to visit our brother Sid in Shreveport. It was love at first sight. He asked her to marry him right away, that same night! Of course she thought he was crazy, but she was interested.

After our Longview honeymoon, Ann and I went back to Freedom, Pennsylvania. We took a long, round-about trip before we found our way back to East Texas.

Both our families lived close together in Freedom. As newlyweds, we were happy to be near them. Both our families were originally from Lithuania. We're Litvaks. We're "herring snappers." We're not Hungars or Galitzianas. The families came from an area near Vilna, so they felt as though they were *landtsmen*, neighbors. That was probably the only reason Ann's family, the Gordons, were willing to accept me.

Both our families were strictly kosher. At least, my family was kosher until my mother had a stroke. Between my dad and the boys, we managed to mix everything up so badly it was just about impossible to put it right again. That was the end of keeping kosher for us.

My mother was serious about religion. There were five rabbis in her family. Not my dad, though. All seven of my father's brothers were butchers and slaughterers in the packing houses. Even my aunt was a butcher! And she was as good one, too. She was famous at a time when it was unheard-of for a woman to be a butcher.

Even though they had a lot in common, our families were very different. To begin with, Ann only had one sister. Her parents, Sarah and Louis Gordon, were extremely polite and proper. My family had four boys and one girl. We had an awful lot of fun, but we were not always so proper or polite.

For instance, we didn't think anything about running around the house in our underwear. The first time I brought Ann to our house, she spent most of the time hiding her head because she never saw her father running around in his underwear. Never! At the Gordons' house, when you got up in the morning you got dressed before you came downstairs to eat breakfast. At our house, you could run around in your underwear all day long if that's what you felt like doing.

My parents, Dora and Sam Balter, had a big three-story house that was connected to our store. We needed that much room because we had so many kids and we always had friends coming and going. Everybody would stop off with us. We had so much company we never knew who was sleeping in our house. Sometimes you would go to your room to go to bed and find some guest sleeping there, so you would have to go find another place to sleep.

We'd all sit down to eat our meals together at a long table. My dad used to check on everything that was going on with the family at that table. Everything happened at our table. The first time Ann came to our house, my dad was seated at the head of the table and my mother was at one side. Then there was my brother Ace, then Benjie, me, Sid, Minnie, and Ann, who was seated in the middle. They were zipping all the food past her and aggravating her. I told her if she didn't grab the food platters when they came past she wasn't going to get anything to eat. I said, "Don't ask for what you want and sit there and wait for it, you'd better reach out and take it!"

During the meal Ann said, "May I have the mashed potatoes?" Ace reached over and took a handful of mashed potatoes and tossed them onto her plate. My mother was furious. She made them stop and she made them behave. They were only teasing Ann because they knew she was a little shy, and because she was so proper.

They weren't doing anything particularly unkind. We did the same thing to our sister Minnie every time she brought a boyfriend home. We ran off a lot of her boyfriends! We didn't have the chance to pick on her husband Milton, though. He only came to see us one time, and that was fifteen minutes before their wedding. They were married on New Year's Day at our aunt Sarah's house in Elwood City, thirty minutes from Freedom. Milton said he had never been so cold in his life.

Ann became sick with diabetes right after our son Gordon was born. She was in the hospital twenty-one times in a period of three years. She never stayed in the hospital for less than three weeks at a time. Of course we had no insurance. It got pretty expensive, and so I had to find a way to earn enough money to pay for all those doctors and hospitals.

Jobs were not plentiful, but I was willing to do anything to support my wife and our baby and pay all those doctor bills. I found out that there was a shortage of firemen and engineers on the railroad. I started working on the railroad runs from the South and West to the East Coast. I'd be gone on an engine several days at a time while Ann and the baby stayed in Freedom with my parents.

I was the fireman who made the steam to make the engine go. We had coal burners. Some engines had stokers, and some had hand-firers. I had an eighteen- or twenty-inch shovel, and I'd shovel for 120 to 200 miles at a time. Many times I'd empty that whole coal bin by myself. You can see pictures that will show you how the coal bin rode behind the engine. You can still see it these days on toy train sets, or in the movies.

The work was hard, but that was not a problem for me. I was young, I was strong, and I was accustomed to working hard. The hard part was being away from Ann and the baby. It made me crazy. I couldn't stand to be away from them. The railroad ran right behind my parents' house, practically in our back yard. When we got near the house I would beg the engineer, "How about stopping here just for a minute? My wife is sick. Let me run in and see her? Let me run in and see my baby?" They'd stop the train, and I would run in and check on Ann and Gordon. On my way out, I'd grab a bunch of snack food from the store for the engineer and I'd jump back on the engine and we'd be gone.

Even though I was making good money, I was away from home too much. I'd be out on an engine and I'd get a message telling me my wife was in the hospital. I never knew how serious her condition was, or how dangerous it was, and I was half a continent away. There was nothing I could do to help her. I couldn't even go to the hospital to see her.

I had to find a way to be home with my family every night, where I could see them and touch them and know they were all right. I bid off the long railroad runs for a job in the yards, shifting trains as they'd come through. When you shift the trains, you take the cars off the train they come in on and add them to the train they need to go out on. For instance, when a train comes into the yard it may have thirty cars bound for Chicago. Those thirty cars are pulled out to go one way. It may have also thirty cars to go to St. Louis. Those cars are pulled out to go a different way. You have to separate them. The engine pushes them up over a hump, and then they cut them off and send them where they want them. I worked in the yards, and I did extra work as a fireman for local trains, but no matter how hard I worked, I couldn't make enough money to pay the doctor bills.

When I finally got enough seniority to be able to choose my hours, I'd go to work at the railroad yard from seven in the morning until three in the afternoon. Then I'd drive to Ambridge, where I worked as a laborer at the A. M. Byers Company, a steel mill, getting the material ready to go into the steel furnaces. I'd work there from four in the afternoon until midnight.

The steel mill had big electric furnaces and three big electrodes to melt the steel. When I'd get my work done, I'd watch the men operate the furnace. I'd watch how much aluminum they'd put in, how much manganese they'd add. Each of those electrodes was so big, a large man couldn't put his arms around it. When they came down, the sparks would fly off and the electricity would melt the steel.

The electrodes normally came down automatically, but sometimes you'd hear a tremendous splash. A piece of steel would fall down and short out against two electrodes to make the splash. You'd have to run over and turn a handle to allow the electrodes to go up and let the steel fall in.

One evening, the guys who worked the furnace were at the other end kibbitzing while the furnace was melting. A bunch of steel fell in and made a hell of a noise, so I ran and hit the key to lift the electrode. It worked and solved the problem. When the men heard the noise, they knew what happened. The melter, the number-one man, came running, but by the time he got there it was all over. I had lifted the electrodes. He looked around and said, "Who did that? Who operated the furnace?"

I didn't know whether I'd done something wrong or not, but I said, "I did it."

He said, "Did you ever work in the furnace before? How did you know what to do?"

I told him, "I learned how to do it by watching you."

Two days later they got me to work on the furnace. They needed extra men, and I was put to work shoveling. That was no big deal for me. I had a lot of experience shoveling coal as a fireman on the trains. There were a lot of Poles working there. They found out I was a Jew and they said, "You're the first Jew we've ever seen who would work this hard. We never heard of a Jew doing hard work. There's never been a Jew who would work in the steel mill before."

I said, "Look, you Pollack bastard, if you'd keep your mouth shut and do some work yourself, we'd all get something done! This Jew came up here to work, so don't bother me. You go your way and I'll go mine. Just stay out of my way and let me do my job."

They laughed and shook my hand. They respected me after that. They knew we could work together and we got along just fine.

It was so hot we would lose ten pounds a day. Anne and I had taken an apartment in a government housing project up on the hill. Gordon was a year old, and when Ann would hear explosions at the steel mill she would be terrified. She would grab Gordon and run to see if the whole place had blown up. I used to tease her about it, but it wasn't unreasonable for her to worry, because accidents happened, and when they happened they were bad.

One time, I did come home all bandaged. The bigshots in Pittsburgh decided they could save themselves some money. Some engineer got the idea of using slag from the rolling mill—that's the stuff they knock off the ingots after they make them, instead of the iron ore we normally used to stir the steel as they made it. It cleans it out and brings the impurities up so that they spill over and run out. What the engineer from Pittsburgh wanted to do was to load the furnaces with a layer of scrap, a layer of slag, a layer of scrap, a layer of slag, and so on.

Our superintendent was an old steel maker from way back. He was a university graduate, but he had common sense as well as book sense. He had the experience of actually making steel on the floor, and he didn't like what they were doing. The day they tried it, the bigshots came down to watch, but the superintendent warned us to be careful. He told us to watch out for anything unusual.

The doors on the furnace were eight inches thick, and they were brick inside. When you let the door down, you had a little hole. There was an iron bar that was eighteen to twenty feet long. We had to pick it up, then bounce it up high enough to stick it through that little hole to loosen the steel so that it would melt. When it melted, it foamed.

We got a real fast meld. I put the bar in to check it. It went down to the bottom all right, but I felt nothing but hard steel. The bottom wasn't melted. I poked the bar around, loosening it, then pulled it out. When you pulled it out, it was so hot that a lot of it came out with the bar, so you had to put it in a water trough to cool. I went back, and just as I pressed the button to lift the door, the whole furnace started to shake.

What happened was that the cold steel came up and hit the hot melted steel and it was starting to boil over! I was standing in front of that door. I had to get out of the way! When it started to blow, everybody ran. I realized that the furnace was still on. I hit the switch to shut it off before I ran. A man who was standing in front of the door with me turned around to look at what was happening. He fell down below the furnace door.

The heat was so intense that if you were within two hundred feet of the thing your ears swelled up. I had a leather jacket hanging on the wall about fifty feet from the furnace. When we went back after it was all over, the heat had shrunk it down to the size of a doll's jacket.

We were badly blistered, but it didn't blow the furnace up completely. The only thing that saved it was that I was lucky enough to get the door open. Because of the door being open, the hot steel didn't blow out.

When they went back to get the man who had fallen, his clothes were so charred they just fell off him. It was a miracle that he survived.

Our superintendent walked over to the bigshots and said, "Look, I didn't approve of the way they were doing this. These men will walk off the job if you continue to do it this way, and I wouldn't blame them. You take that engineer of yours and you go back to Pittsburgh with him!"

After that, Ann's father decided it was too dangerous for me to work in the mill, so he forced me into the grocery business. I didn't want to go into the grocery business. I wanted to go into some kind of selling, but Mr. Gordon didn't really care what I wanted. He thought he knew what was best for me.

We went for a ride and drove past a store. He asked if I liked that store and I said, "It looks like a nice store." He said, "I'm glad you like it. It's yours." He had bought it for me.

What could I do? I couldn't refuse such a generous gift. I worked for a while and built the business up. I hated it. I could have sold it two or three times for a really good price, but Ann's father wouldn't let me sell it. He knew my sister and brothers were living in Texas, and he wanted to tie us down close to him in Pennsylvania. He didn't want Ann to move away. He was afraid to lose his daughter.

I stood it as long as I could, but it finally came to a head. A young boy who worked for me lived in a foster home down the street. He was a good, hardworking kid, and I liked him. A woman who lived across the street would come in every day to buy two loaves of bread and a quart of milk. When the boy saw her hit the door, he got the milk and bread and had them waiting for her. She started shouting at him for "assuming" what she wanted to buy. She was really horrible to him. I walked up to her and I said, "Look, I make two cents on this and I make three cents on that. I don't want your three cents and I don't want your two cents. Go out the door right now and forget about shopping here. Don't ever come back."

That did it. I sat down and wrote a check to pay my butcher. I paid the kid. I locked the door and went straight to my father-in-law's business. I said, "I came to give you the store. Here's the key. You wouldn't let me sell it, so now you can have it. You can take all the merchandise. It's triple the stock that was in it before you bought it for me. I don't want any part of it."

All he could say was, "What kind of a thing is that for a Jewish boy to do?"

We certainly didn't make any money on that deal.

The very next week, my sister Minnie came home to Freedom. She needed help back in Texas. Her husband, Milton, made a bad deal and got hung up with a bunch of bad whiskey he bought from some ex-Capone man out of Chicago. Milton was always finding something to make a deal about; that's the kind of guy he was. Milton had this letter of credit up for it. They were trying to sell the whiskey around East Texas, but nobody would buy it.

My sister needed help, so I came to Texas to help her. In a little more than two months I sold over a million and a half dollars' worth of bad whiskey for her.

Ann cried for weeks after we came to Texas. We had to say good-bye to everyone and everything we knew and cared about. She was homesick. She missed her family, her parents and her sister, and she missed our friends, our town. Plus, she was physically sick. My brother Ace and his wife Iris had moved into a nice little house here. They decided we should have the house because we had a child. Gordon was small, Ann wasn't well, and they thought maybe if we had the house we could adjust more comfortably to living here. We lived in that house for quite a while, and it helped. After that, we lived in the first prefabricated house in town. Milton had it shipped in here on a railroad car.

Milton was in the beer business, and I worked for him. We delivered beer in Kilgore and all over East Texas. There was a place called "Honkey Tonk City" in the area where the bridge over the Sabine River and I-20 now come together. There were a bunch of little screen-door honkey tonks down there. They were rough! They were wild! They used to have a killing every night. If you'd wait ten minutes you'd see at least one fight. There was always somebody drunk and shooting.

There used to be row after row of honkey tonks along the Kilgore Highway. The first time I saw Elvis Presley, I was delivering beer to one of the honkey tonks out there and this nice-looking kid was up on the stage practicing whatever it was he did, shaking and screaming and yelling. I thought, Who is that crazy SOB? I didn't know who he was then, but it was Elvis Presley.

Milton also got me involved in bootlegging. The state of Oklahoma was dry. While it was against Oklahoma law to transport liquor from Texas to Oklahoma, it wasn't dry as far as federal law was concerned. We had an import and export license, so there was some question about whether what we were doing was actually illegal. One thing for sure, the officials in Oklahoma thought it was illegal.

We had a C-47, and our pilot used to fly into Oklahoma every other day. I rode copilot. The pilot taught me how to put the gears up and down, put the flaps up and down. We would land and unload the booze into the bootlegger's waiting trucks. Or we would land and unload it into our own truck and then run a truckload through Oklahoma—until the time we got hijacked, and then we quit.

One day we went to see a bootlegger in Anadarko, Oklahoma. We were going to land in a field; from the air, it looked like there was a ditch running through the field, but it was only a pipeline underground. The pilot made a couple of swipes at the field, and by the time we landed, the whole city was out there waiting for us, police and all. The police asked us where we were going. We said, "We fly flowers and orchids to the East Coast from California, but we wanted to stop and see somebody who lived here who was in the army with us."

So we took off and we went to the bootlegger's house. We figured we were safe doing that, since nobody was left in town. They were all out at the field. He was hiding. He said, "You're crazy, coming in here like that!" He told us about another field, and we landed there a couple of times. We used to land in an old airport at downtown Oklahoma City, unload, take off again, and fly out to the big airport.

Our last flight was something else altogether. We arrived at the landing site and saw the trucks waiting to load the whiskey. We landed. They came out and loaded the whiskey. When they were all loaded, the truck drivers came over to us and flashed their badges. They were state troopers! They said, "We have your whiskey as evidence, and we have all the evidence we need to put you away, but we are going to let you go this time. Just don't ever come back to Oklahoma or you are going to go to jail." It wasn't exactly a hijacking, since they were state troopers, but they took our merchandise and gave us nothing, so it turned out that we were hijacked by the

Law. We felt lucky that they let us go, so we took them at their word and we didn't ever go back.

There was a real hijacking, too. Thankfully, I wasn't there the day the truck got hijacked, but I often drove the bootleg truck. It was fixed up to look like an oil truck. It was once a real oil truck, but they cut the guts out of it. They kept a thin layer of oil around the outside. If somebody questioned the driver, he could turn the tap and real oil would come out so there wouldn't be any problems. The whiskey was camouflaged inside.

When I drove the truck for a long way, sometimes I would be too tired to go on, so I'd stop at a courthouse to rest. I figured it was the safest place to be. Nobody was going to bother me at the courthouse. I'd pull up in front of the courthouse, go inside, and tell them I was driving a load of oil across the state and I was too tired to drive safely. I'd ask if it would be all right if I parked in front of the courthouse and slept for a while. I asked if they would look out for me while I was sleeping to make sure nobody bothered me. They were always very nice and friendly, and they would say, "Sure. Pull up right over here." So I'd take a nap, and then I'd get up and go on my way.

I didn't make any money on that deal, either.

While we were flying whiskey into Oklahoma I became frightened because it was dangerous and I didn't want to leave my wife and child penniless if something happened to me. Every time I'd go up I'd think I was never going to see my family again. I didn't know anything about insurance back then, so I went to see Mayor G. A Bodenheim because he was the insurance man who sold insurance to all the Jews in town. Thank goodness my family never had to rely on it, because that insurance didn't cover me when I was flying in an airplane. Later, when I went into the insurance business I was always careful to see that my clients got exactly what they needed.

"Bodie" was originally a cotton broker who came here when cotton was a big product in this area. He was Jewish, although his wife was Christian. He never converted, but he raised his sons, Edwin and Roland, as Christians. He was closely related to the Bodenheimer family in Shreveport, although they remained Jewish and his family did not. He was not alone. There are a lot of old families in Longview and in East Texas who were originally Jewish but who are now Christians.

Bodenheim's office was upstairs in the old Everett Bank building where the Gregg County Historical Museum is now located. You had to go up steep, narrow steps to get there.

Bodie had a temper. One time, Bodie got mad at Carl Estes, the newspaper publisher, and he called him on the phone. Bodie said, "I'll wait for you in front of the bank building. You come down here, and I'll kill you!" Bodie was pacing up and down the street in front of the bank with his carnation in his lapel and a gun in his hand, waiting for Carl Estes to show up so he could kill him. Of course, Carl Estes knew better than to appear. Bodie was a little guy, but a man with a gun is as big as anyone else.

Bodie was smart, personable, and political. He was so well liked that he was elected mayor of Longview. When he died, both a Rabbi and a Christian minister conducted the service, and the whole town turned out.

At first, the only friends Ann and I had here were members our family. My sister and brother-in-law, Minnie and Milton Galoob, and my brother and sister-in-law, Ace and Iris Balter, were our closest relatives and our closest friends. We always went to my sister Minnie's house in the evenings, since she never wanted to go out to anybody else's house.

Minnie and Milton had a knack for making people feel comfortable. We had poker games and dinners, and we would visit each other all the time. We'd go to the movies. We'd go out to the T&P Café for coffee. The T&P Café was only a little hole-in-the-wall coffee shop across the street from the railroad station, but it was someplace to go. You'd sit there drinking your coffee and listening to the trains come into town.

We'd go dancing at Mattie's Ballroom. Mattie would bring in the big bands, like Harry James and Benny Goodman. Milton's sister, Celia Bergman, and her wealthier crowd had really elegant parties. For some reason we were always invited to their parties. Ann tells me it's because they never knew what I was going to say or do next.

The Sam Dorfmans had a big house with pillars in front and a swimming pool in back. They invited us to a swimming party. That's the first time I'd ever seen a place like that! They had maids running around serving mint juleps. I went home and thought, "Boy, that's what it's like to live in high cotton!"

The first time we went to a dinner party at Etta and Morris Sosland's house, she served gefilte fish on one side of the table and a big ham on the other. I never saw anything like that before, either. Gefilte fish and ham? I couldn't believe it! Celia and Dave Bergman used to have Passover Seders and other holidays at their house, and we went there.

We went to Temple in Kilgore. I wound up being the official Shofar (ram's horn) blower because nobody else could blow the thing. They had a little Shofar, and since they never could get any sound out of it, they just did without it until I came along. I was young and strong, so I picked it up and blew the hell out of it.

Ben Antwell was hard of hearing. His hearing aids came out of his eyeglasses into his ears. The first time I blew Shofar on the High Holidays at the Kilgore Temple, Ben was sitting in the second row. I walked up to the Bimah (dais) and started blowing the Shofar. I saw Ben reaching into his ears and pulling like crazy. After it was over he walked up to me and said, "You almost blew my head off!" After that, when I'd get up to go to the Bimah, the men would play like they were trying to stop me.

We used to have two services. One was an early-morning service for the old-timers who wanted to continue a more Orthodox tradition, and the other was a dignified Reform service for the rest of the congregation.

I'd blow the Shofar for the early service as well as for the Reform service. One morning, for some reason, I had a terrible time. I'd blow and blow and no decent sound would come out. That's not unusual. Shofarim are unpredictable and stubborn. It happens sometimes, and there's really no good scientific explanation for it. In fact, a whole history of legends, superstitions, and bubbameisas (old wives' tales) has grown up about why the Shofar wouldn't blow. Sometimes they say a little devil has crawled into it and won't let the holy notes come out.

That day Mr. Leibson said, "What's the matter with you? Why don't you blow it? Give it some strength!"

I told him, "I'll tell you the truth, Mr. Leibson, I ate prunes last night, and I was afraid of what would happen if I would give it a good blow . . ."

He got hysterical laughing. He sat up in the front row with a couple of the other old men. All during the regular service, when I got up to blow the Shofar, they sat there with these big smiles on their faces, trying to make me laugh so that I couldn't blow the Shofar at all.

I would practice blowing the Shofar while I was driving from Longview to the Temple in Kilgore. It was so loud in the car that the sound could drive you crazy. I got pretty good on it and I had built up a big repertoire of songs for my "concerts." I could even play "Jingle Bells" and "Silent Night" on the Shofar.

When we found ourselves between rabbis, the members of the congregation took turns doing services. One Friday night it was my turn to do the service, and Mr. Leibson was once again sitting in the first row. He came up to me after the service and asked, " Are you Jewish?"

"Of course," I answered.

"Are you REALLY Jewish?"

"Of course."

I was butchering the Hebrew so badly that he said, "You know, after listening to you, I don't think you're Jewish!"

He was not alone. Our whole family came to our son Gordon's Bar Mitzvah in Kilgore. We had a house full of company and we were nervous. We were halfway to Kilgore when someone said, "Oh, my! We forgot Gordon!" We had to drive all the way back to Longview to get the guest of honor!

It was a beautiful Bar Mitzvah. Our son did really well, and we were all proud of him. My father-in-law kept looking at him, though, and shaking his head in disbelief. He'd lean over to me and say, "I know he's praying, but what language is he praying in? It doesn't sound like Hebrew to me!" Gordon's Texas accent made the Hebrew words sound strange to his grandfather.

In many ways, being a Jew in the oilpatch was different from being a Jew in Pennsylvania. In many ways it was the same. Jews involved in the oil business included Dorfman, Felsenthal, and Florsheim, who worked for Dorfman. My cousin Ben Balter was a good land man and did a lot of leasing for a lot of people. He would tell us how H. L. Hunt used to hide out in a field he had on the other side of Kilgore, headed toward New London. Hunt had a lease and he had a little shack up in the middle of the pasture. From that shack, he could see anyone who was coming toward him, and if it was somebody he owed money, as he often did, he'd go somewhere else and hide. Hunt slept in back of Hymie Hurwitz's men's clothing store in Kilgore many a night.

In order to get into the oil business, a person has to go out and find a lease. That's the land you drill on. If you're promoting it, you have to find people who will buy into it. If you can do it yourself, you're better off because you don't have to worry. If it's a dry hole you're not a thief, you haven't taken somebody else's money for nothing. If it hits, you're a good boy. If it doesn't hit, you're a thief. It's a gamble. You've got to be willing to take a chance. Many oilmen got their start by owing everybody money. Even today, when guys are promoting, they'll drill a well, but they'll shoot it into two different zones. One zone belongs to the investors, and one zone is all theirs.

Bernard Davis's brother had drilled some wells in Texas, east of San Marcos. They were shallow wells with good production. So Bernard and I went in together. We got some fellows to go with us, and we drilled a dry hole. We hit a fault and we were in the wrong side of it. After it was all over, Bernard went down to Tullos, Louisiana, and put in a supply store.

He told me there was an area down there where you could drill old leases and get production. I found a fellow who had some leases he wanted to get rid of, but he wanted to do the drilling. I asked Milton if he wanted to go in with me, and that's how we happened to find our way to Tullos, Louisiana. It turned out to be another one of those deals I didn't make any money on.

A lot has happened since Ann and I came to visit my cousins in Texas on our honeymoon. East Texas grows on you. There have been deals we didn't make money on, and deals we did, but the most important thing is that we made a lot of friends along the way. Good friends are better than wealth, because people who have good friends are the richest people of all.

CHAPTER 5

Celia Bergman

"The oilfield lights were just a-going like fire! They were diamonds in the sky!"

It may sound strange to say I was raised in the lap of luxury after the rough beginnings of following the oil booms from town to town along the railroad line. It was not always easy, but there wasn't anything I ever wanted that I couldn't have.

When I was in college I visited Oklahoma City, where I bought myself a fur coat and wrote a personal check for it. That same day I bought a grand piano and wrote a personal check for it, as well. I wasn't what you would call spoiled, but it was nice to have everything I wanted in those good days before the stock market crash.

I was born in Passaic, New Jersey. When I was three years old, my mother and father moved to Philadelphia. My last name was Kins. My brother Jack and I were the two children Mama had with my father. We lived in Philadelphia until my father died, when I was seven and a half years old.

Mama had two brothers who lived in the Oklahoma Territory, and she decided to join them. A young widow with no one to guide or protect her, she picked up her two kids, got on the train, and off we went to Oklahoma!

I can remember the day they buried my father, but I can't remember anything about that trip to Oklahoma. We traveled by train because there were no planes or cars. After all, that was a long time ago. Amazingly, we did find her brothers in that wild Oklahoma Territory. Mama opened a small variety store in Oklahoma City, and we lived in an apartment with a bedroom and a kitchen and a little living room in back of the store. It was not unusual for people to live like that.

My mother later met and married Dave Galoob, and we went on to live in a variety of small towns in Oklahoma. The Frisco Railroad ran as a straight shoot from Tulsa to Oklahoma City. They would be drilling for oil at all the railroad stops, and my folks would follow the railroad and open a store wherever there was a new oilfield. It was a difficult life, but they worked hard and they were successful with it.

I wanted to go to college, but we were living in Paydon, Oklahoma, where the high school was not accredited. Since I could not attend an unaccredited high school, my family allowed me to live with my mother's cousin and go to school in Oklahoma City. My mother's cousin had just come to America. She couldn't speak a

Religious studies and Confirmation have always been an important part of life in the Jewish community. These three proud young confirmants were dressed up to celebrate their happy occasion. Right to left: Harriet Balter, Danny Felsenthal, and Debbie Galoob.
—Photo courtesy of Sandi Sachnowitz

word of English, and I couldn't speak a word of Yiddish. But I learned Yiddish and she learned English, and we got along beautifully.

I graduated from Central High School in Oklahoma City and went to the University of Oklahoma at Norman. They only had four thousand scholars. Of these, there were four Jewish boys and three Jewish girls. I was invited to join the Kappa Kappa Gamma Sorority, but when they found out I was Jewish they rescinded the invitation bid. It was a cruel thing for them to do, but that's the way people were at the time. I didn't really care. I wasn't interested in those kinds of things. The four Jewish boys at the university were very lovely to the Jewish girls. We became our own little college family.

As I was finishing my second year of college, my mother took terribly ill with what the doctors then called "rheumatism." All they could do was advise her to take hot baths and use hot packs for her knees. Mama couldn't walk, and Sarah, Milton, and Reva were still young, so I had to come home to take care of the kids. That killed my hopes for college, but the important thing was that Mama did get a little better and I went on to get married.

How I met my husband Dave is the funniest thing you ever heard in your life. It's hard to believe it because it is a story straight from heaven!

When I was nineteen, I was doing all the ready-to-wear buying for our three stores. I was in Kansas City on a buying trip. My college friend Rose, from Atokah, Oklahoma, had just married and was living in Saint Joseph, Missouri. There was an Interurban car from Kansas City to Saint Jo, so I called her and invited her and her husband to come have dinner with me. She said, "Celia, we just got back from our honeymoon today. My folks gave me a new Cord Automobile for a wedding gift, and I want you to see it. You come here and spend the evening with us, and we'll put you on the Interurban so you can go back tonight."

She didn't tell me she was going to get me a date, but Dave was my blind date because she thought he was perfect for me. He thought so, too. He fell in love with me right away, but I was practically engaged to a fellow from St. Louis who was a manufacturer of silk comforts. Silk comforts were an elegant and popular household item. My folks encouraged the relationship because even though he was ten years older than me, he was a nice man with a lot of money and they knew he would provide for me and take care of me.

The Balter and Galoob families in Longview. L-R, front row: Ann Balter, Milton Galoob, Minnie Balter, Iris Balter, Rae Balter; back row: Norman Balter, Minnie Galoob Balter, Benjie Balter, Ace Balter, and Sid Balter.

—Photo courtesy Gordon Balter

I didn't exactly fall in love with Dave right away, but I liked him a lot and I knew he made me happy. I sent him a card when the High Holy Days came in September. I sent the card to Missouri. His father mailed it to him in Tulsa, Oklahoma. He called me and said, "Can I come to see you for the holiday?"

We were living in Sepalpa, only forty miles from Tulsa, so I said, "We don't have a Temple here. We have nothing to offer you for the High Holy Days, so I'll have to come to Tulsa to see you." And I went. He was living with his aunt and uncle. When his aunt met me, she started pushing our relationship.

That train from Sepalpa to Tulsa went straight on to St. Louis, so we ran away to St. Louis and got married in the rabbi's study in the St. Louis Reform Temple. The afternoon of our wedding, we left for St. Joseph, Missouri, where Dave's father and sister lived.

My folks were not exactly happy when they found out what we had done, but they accepted it. I really think Mama knew what I was doing. We ran away because my folks didn't want me to marry Dave—not because they didn't like him, but because he didn't have any money and the other fellow did. They weren't being greedy or inconsiderate or any of the things you might think. It was the depression, and life was uncertain. They simply wanted me to have a secure life.

We were married in 1931. Times were hard, and Dave was always out on the road, selling hats and caps. The man who owned the silk comfort factory could have given me all the finer things in life which I was accustomed to. But I loved Dave. I knew I'd have a good life with him. And I never regretted my decision. My husband was the best person there ever was. We had a wonderful life together, and I have lovely memories.

After Dave and I married, my folks opened a store for us in Bristow, where we lived for three years. Then we went to Shawnee. We sold the Shawnee store before we came to Longview in February 1931.

We'd gone fishing in Hot Springs, Arkansas, when my mother called to tell us that my brother, Jack Kins, who owned a store in Kilgore, was terribly sick with malaria and was all alone in that town with nobody to look after him. Mama said, "You'd better get to Kilgore and see about Jack." I said, "Okay, Mama, I'm on my way," and we left the Arlington Hotel and started out immediately.

When we came through Longview that night, the mud was at least eighteen inches deep and the oilfield lights were just a-going like fire! They were diamonds in the sky! You have never seen anything like it! I told Dave, "I like this town."

"What do you like about it, the noise or the mud?" he asked.

I said, "I like it all."

Jack was feeling a little better by the time we got to Kilgore, but I really liked the area, and so I said, "Dave, let's stay in Longview for a few days." That was okay with him. So we started looking for a business location.

But it was the start of the oil boom, and you couldn't rent a spot for love nor money. We heard there was a drugstore going bankrupt downtown, but of course everybody in the world was trying to get the location. There were nine heirs to that little twenty-five-foot building. People said they were impossible to deal with, but Dave made up his mind he was going to get that building, and when Dave made up his mind to do something, he usually did it. Dave was a charmer. He went to see those people about that building every day for ten days, until he finally convinced them to let him have it.

We called our business "Martin's" and we knew we were going to carry really lovely, top-quality ladies' clothing. But first, we had to find a place to live. Living locations were even scarcer than business locations. We stayed at the old hotel downtown for three or four months. It was acceptable, but it wasn't all that comfortable. We were finally able to rent a lovely bedroom with a private bath in the Walker home.

"You'd normally have to be here ten years before folks in this town would accept you," Mrs. Walker told me. "We old-timers are very particular about who we accept into our homes, but I like you and I'm going to let you live here." She charged us eighty-five dollars a month, which was a lot of money, but we felt lucky to get it because not only was it cheaper than the hotel, but it was a whole lot nicer, too.

We stayed there about a year while everything we owned was in storage. Eventually we needed a roomier place to live, so we built a beautiful three-bedroom, two-bathroom bungalow on Houston Street. You might not think it was elegant by today's standards, but it was a lovely home for the time.

We became close friends with Sam Dorfman, a Jewish oilman who lived across from us on Houston Street. He was married to Rose Gold from Shreveport, but they eventually divorced and he later married Elizabeth. Sam and Elizabeth had two awfully nice boys, Sam Jr. and Louis.

By the time we were thinking of building another house, Sam had moved to an elegant white two-story house on Sylvan Drive. He wanted us for his neighbors, and he was accustomed to having what he wanted. But the price for the lot was two thousand dollars—a fortune in those days! Dave told Sam he didn't have the money.

Sam said, "I'll buy it and you'll pay me when you have the money." Dave wouldn't agree to that, but Sam just bought the lot right then and there. And he bought it in Dave's name.

You could barely count all the millionaires in the Christian community of Longview because there were so many of them, but Sam Dorfman was our only Jewish millionaire at that time. He had oil interests, and a pipe yard and oilfield supplies.

Dave and I worked hard, but we always managed to go home for

The happy family poses before the Ark of Temple Beth Sholom in Kilgore in celebration of Sam Galoob's Bar Mitsvah. Right to left: Minnie Galoob, Sam's twin sister, Sandi Galoob, Rebecca Galoob, Milton Galoob, Sam Galoob, and Debbie Galoob.

—Photo courtesy of Sandi Sachnowitz

lunch and for the evening meal. I always had help at home, even when we didn't have five cents in our pockets. I worked in the store, and I couldn't do both the store work and housework.

You could get good help for fifteen to eighteen dollars a week during the oil boom. I know that sounds low, but it was relative. We didn't earn much, and so we couldn't pay our help much, but we could all get by on very little. Eggs were nineteen cents a dozen.

Bread was ten cents a loaf. Everybody was happy to have work, no matter what kind of work it might be.

A year after we opened the store, my sister Sarah came to help us. She lived with us until she married Eddie Picow in 1940 and moved away to South Carolina. Later, my mother and my sister Reva came to Longview and we bought them a nice home.

Dave and I had built a beautiful ladies' ready-to-wear store with fine merchandise and a reputation for elegance, in the same category as Neiman Marcus in Dallas. People came from all over East Texas, western Louisiana, and southern Oklahoma to shop with us.

Even though we were successful, Dave hated the retail business. The pressure was too much for him, and he felt that the pressure was too much for me as well, so he insisted that we retire very young. Dave was only sixty, and I was only fifty. He said he'd rather have ten thousand dollars less a year and live a longer time. And that's what happened.

My mother was furious and wouldn't speak to me for weeks! She felt that we were giving up a gold mine.

I didn't want to retire at first, and I refused to sign the papers. But my husband turned to me and said, "Do you want to be the richest widow in Longview? That's what you are going to be if you don't let me sell this store." When he said that, I just told him, "Go ahead and sell out."

He always said that Longview was good to him, and he was good to it. He said, "You can't just take things out of a city, you have to put back as much or more than you take." That was his philosophy, and he was well known for his community work. He was one of the original members of the Longview Planning and Zoning Commission. He was a hard worker for the Boy Scouts, who gave him such high honors as the "Silver Beaver" Award and the "Antelope" Award. He was president of the East Texas Tuberculosis Association, member of the board of directors of the Good Shepherd Medical Center, and member of the board or executive committee of just about everything else worthwhile in this town. Everybody in town admired him and loved him.

About the time that we retired, my brother Jack Kins was just getting into the oil business. Although we were comfortable, I knew we wouldn't be able to live the way I wanted to live. So I called Jack and said, "I know you don't need my money, but I'd like to have an

Dave Bergman and a good friend.
—Photo courtesy of Sandi Sachnowitz

interest in the oil business you're starting because I don't think I've got quite enough to live on for the rest of my life. I'd like to take a chance. I want you to take me in." He agreed. We were lucky.

From the day we moved here, Dave and I belonged to the Civic Music Association, but that was all there was in terms of a cultural life. There wasn't that much to do for entertainment during the oil boom.

After the first three or four years, we created a nice social life for ourselves. About fifteen Jewish couples had parties all the time. Every other Sunday night there was either a spaghetti supper or a dinner at one of the homes. The men would play poker and the women would play bridge. We all entertained nicely.

The whole group went out together, and you had a good time when you went out dancing at Mattie's Ballroom, which later became the Rio Palm Isle. All the big bands in the nation came through Longview and played at Mattie's. It wasn't what you'd call a "nice" place, but it was a lot more respectable than you might think.

Our group didn't often socialize with Christian people. We weren't snobby or cliquish, and we certainly didn't feel that we were not welcomed by our Christian neighbors. There were a great many lovely, likeable, gracious Christian people here, and we did visit with them in the civic work that we did. But we enjoyed our own company and they enjoyed theirs.

During the early days of the boom, there was no Temple in Longview, but Marshall had the well-established Reform Temple Moses Montefiore, a beautiful Temple with a beautiful choir, and they always had a Rabbi. That's where Dave and I always went

Unfortunately, most of the Jewish people there were snobs. The people from Longview would go there for Yom Kippur, and we would stay in town all day long and not one of them would invite us into their homes. Of course we didn't want to travel back and forth on the bad roads between the morning and afternoon services, but nobody would invite us to their homes, so we'd go to the hotel and sit in the lobby until the services started again. I never could understand why they were the way they were. We paid our dues. We were members. We belonged, but we were always treated as outsiders.

There was one really lovely person in Marshall, though. Adele Kariel, Mrs. Louis Kariel Sr., was as beautiful inside as she was outside. Gentle, kind, and sweet to everyone, she was one of the few Marshall people who tried to be pleasant to us.

Although we made a point to attend High Holy Day and holiday services in Marshall, we couldn't attend regular Friday-night services, because the roads were so bad. Today you can make the trip to Marshall in about thirty-five minutes, but it used to take much longer during the oil boom.

It's hard to remember all the people who lived here and moved away. There was a Mr. Packman who was Joe Riff's partner when he opened his store. The K. Wolens store was managed by Mannie Franks, who came here with his wife Evelyn and their son and daughter. In 1931, they brought Bernie Weinstein from Cincinnatti. He and his wife Ruth had one daughter, Terrie, a beautiful child with lots of pretty blond curls. Louis Bernstein also worked for K-Wolens.

There was a man named Katz. He and his partner, Frank Seliger, came from El Dorado, Arkansas, to open the KC Store. Frank and Hilda Seliger and their two sons, Maurice and Lewis, rented a house on Green Street where the Sosland family later lived with their sons, Leonard and Jay.

I will never forget Mrs. Miller, who owned the New York Dress Store. She used to sit on a chair near the door and watch everything that happened on the street. She knew everything that was going on in town—and there was quite a lot going on.

Israel and Sophie Futoransky had a grocery store near the Rita Theater. Sophie was my cousin. My mother held Sophie in her arms all the way across the ocean when they traveled in steerage from Europe in 1895. My mother was only fourteen years old and my cousin Sophie was only eighteen months old when they made the trip. The Futoranskys' daughter Sylvia was married at the Temple in Marshall. Their son Harry moved to Hobbs, New Mexico, and their daughter Iris became famous as the director of the Alley Theater in Houston. We were all shocked when she was brutally murdered there.

My brother Milton Galoob came to East Texas because I was here. After he came to Longview, my sister Sarah came, then my mother Rebecca Kins Galoob and my baby sister Reva.

There were six or seven older ladies living in town. Mrs. Riff was Joe Riff's mother; Mrs. Leibson, whose husband Morris was a tailor; Mrs. Blatt, whose sons, Sidney and Maurice, had Blatt's Women's

Ready-to-Wear store; Mrs. Booken, whose husband was partners with Izzy Levinson in the scrap business; Molly Blatt's mother, Mrs. Fensen; and my mother, Mrs. Galoob. The ladies were very good friends, but they never called each other by their first names. They were always formal, saying Mrs. this or Mrs. that.

Every two weeks they'd come to each other's homes to play bingo. They'd serve coffee and fruit, but not any sweets, because at least half of them were diabetic. When they played bingo one would always blame the others and say that they were cheating. Dave would pick them all up and take them wherever they were playing bingo, and then he would call for them and take them home. It took up a lot of his time, but he did it because Mama wanted him to do it.

A lot of people will tell you that the oil boom was exciting. It may have been exciting for them, but it was hard work for us. The exciting part was that we'd open the store at nine o'clock in the morning and we wouldn't leave until ten o'clock at night. That went on for seven or eight years. We came here during the depression, and we came "COD," cash-on-delivery. Everybody came that way. We didn't have any money, but we were young, we had our health and strength, and we made it.

CHAPTER 6

Phillip Brin

"We saw many a starving person sitting in the open doors of the freight cars as the trains passed through town. All sorts of people were desperate during the depression."

I came to Longview on August 1, 1935. To be perfectly honest, I came here because I couldn't get a job elsewhere. I had graduated with a degree in law from the University of Texas and gone home to Terrell. I stayed there most of the summer, and the only legal work I had was some free title examination for a carpenter friend of my family's.

I was attracted to Longview because of the oil boom. There was a lot to learn about oilfield law, and there was a lot to do. I went to work for Angus Wynne, who had been a lawyer in Kaufman County before he came here. The first paycheck I received was fifteen dollars. In those days, you were so happy to have any sort of job that you didn't demand to know in advance what you were going to be paid.

It was not as bad as it might sound. It didn't cost much to live if you could manage to come by the few pennies you needed. You could buy a malted milk for fifteen cents, or a milkshake for ten cents. We saw many a starving person sitting in the open doors of the freight cars as the trains passed through town. Sometimes we'd see them on the streets hunting a handout. All sorts of people were desperate during the depression.

Phillip Brin at a celebration.
—Photo courtesy of Ada Milstein

One of the most important concerns for a young single man was finding something decent to eat. Horace Young was in charge of the soda fountain at Oliver's drugstore. I ate breakfast there for twenty cents. That included toast and eggs, sausage or ham, and coffee. I could get by on very little money all week, and I would go home to Terrell on the weekends and fill up on that good home-cooked food.

There was a place called the East Texas Cafe, and there was Miss Leila Wood's drugstore in front of the courthouse. For fifteen cents you could get a bowl of Mrs. Leila Wood's homemade chili, with all the crackers and ketchup you wanted. For another fifteen cents she gave you a slice of the best lime pie that you've ever put in your mouth.

At lunchtime we would eat at the Hollywood Cafe. You got a marvelous meal for twenty-five cents. If you wanted steak, your meal was as high as fifty cents, but very few of us could afford to eat steak. For twenty-five cents you would have soup and salad, meat, vegetables, cornbread, biscuits or rolls, and you got iced tea or coffee to drink. You even got a dessert. The food was excellent, and to see Jimmy Brannon prepare it was a treat. He did everything on a griddle in front of you. When he cooked, it was a marvelous production. You got a show as well as a meal. I first met Celia Bergman sitting at the counter at the Hollywood Cafe.

One day, Sam Goldman, an iron and scrap dealer who was in the pipe and supply business in Kilgore, was in Longview trying to collect money for Kilgore's new little Congregation Beth Sholom. Sam saw me in the lobby of the old First National Bank Building. Knowing that I was Jewish, he tackled me and asked me to join the congregation. He said it was just eighteen dollars a year. Even then, eighteen dollars a year didn't sound like much money, so I joined.

At first, Temple Beth Sholom was Conservative. The men and the women did not sit together during services, but they soon voted to become Reform. The building was located on a street near Kilgore College that is now part of the campus. The membership included families from Longview, Kilgore, Gladewater, Overton, and Henderson.

The other big concern for a single young man was finding a decent place to live. People were no longer sleeping on the courthouse lawn, but Longview was crowded. It was still almost impossible to find a place to live. I came here in August and this was the hottest place on earth. Two other young lawyers and I moved into the Longview Arms apartment building downtown. We smelled everybody's food cooking in the crowded little apartments with their low ceilings and small windows. There was no air-conditioning, and you took a sweat bath every night when you came home from work. It was abominable!

Mr. Jim Cockrell was a salesmen for the Longhorn Cement Company who was also from Terrell. He was staying at Mrs. J. O. Mundy's. Mrs. Mundy had several men staying at her house. She checked on you, and you had to meet her qualifications before you could stay there. Hers was a big home with high ceilings. The breezes came through the large windows so that you could be comfortable. I left my two lawyer friends and moved to Mrs. Mundy's. They soon followed me there.

Jim Cockrell had a Studebaker car, and I would frequently ride back and forth to Terrell with him. When the weather was threatening, we rode the train. It rained all the time in those years, and the rain turned the roads to mud. We didn't have mud problems in Longview proper, but we had them on the roads on the way into Longview. Sometimes the road to Kilgore was closed because the Sabine River came up over the road. And this was even after it was paved!

Highway 80 was not paved all the way from Dallas to Longview. At times it would flood. One time, when the Sabine backed up between Gladewater and Big Sandy, it was highly doubtful that even the train would get through. The train had to go through water, and there was a question about whether or not they could do it. The Iron Bridge Dam on Lake Tawakoni solved that problem.

It was an exciting time to be here, and I slowly began to meet the Jewish people. Sam Dorfman would occasionally come into the office because Mr. Wynne represented him. The Sklars and the Dorfmans were clients. Sam Siegel was Mr. Sklar's brother-in-law. The three of them were in the junk business in Shreveport, and they got into the iron and supply business, buying pipe at Shreveport, Louisiana, and El Dorado, Arkansas. They found there was more money in the oil business, and they gradually went from the scrap metal business to the pipe business to the oil business.

When the East Texas oil boom started, drillers needed second-hand pipe. Nobody had any money, so Sam Sklar, Sam Dorfman, and a man named Sam Gold operated what was known as the Louisiana Iron and Supply Company. Later, Sklar and Dorfman bought the Gold family out.

When he first came here, Ben Balter worked for Sklar and Dorfman. That's where he learned the oil business. Ben told me they hired him at twenty-five dollars a week because he had some training in law school and they could ask him as many legal questions as they liked and they didn't have to pay him any legal fees.

I've heard it said that Sonnel Felsenthal, who was in the oil business, wanted to borrow one hundred dollars from the First National Bank and they refused him. He went to the Longview National, which was then called Rembert National, and borrowed his hundred dollars. During the oil boom, the First National Bank would loan money on cattle, but not on oil property. They were afraid of these "irresponsible" oil people.

People came here from all over, Louisana, Oklahoma, and every place you can imagine. The biggest part of the Jewish group here was either in the retail business or the scrap metal or pipe and supply business. There was the Davis family from Tulsa. Al Brown was their nephew, and so was Arthur Arnold. Morris Rudman was in Longview. The Rudman family at Tyler had a place in Longview because of the oil boom.

Several of our people lived in Gladewater. The Sanovs, Morris Levinson and his family, and Ben Scrinovsky, who operated a liquor store. Sam Hurwitz had his store in Gladewater, and his sister Ann Antwell and her husband Ben Antwell helped him. The Antwells' two children, Charles and Jerrell, grew up in in Gladewater.

Izzy Maritsky had a men's clothing store on the block where the Gregg County Historical Museum is now located. Leon Gans had a men's clothing store, and they were competitors. Later, the Hurwitzes acquired what was known as the "Old Stuckey Corner" opposite the post office and the courthouse, and they built a men's clothing store. Hurwitz and Maritsky handled finer lines. Leon was more moderately priced.

There were other Jewish merchants in town, of course. Bernie Weinstein managed The K. Wolens store. Abe Silverman was in the shoe business. The Soslands had an elegant jewelry store. The town stayed open until ten, eleven, twelve o'clock on a Saturday night. That was typical of what merchants did in small towns all over Texas. The country people came into town on Saturday, and they made a day of it.

My father was in the general merchandise business in Terrell. He would be lucky if he got home by eleven o'clock on Saturday night. In fact, when my father went to Dallas on buying trips, he spent a lot of time with the three Statman brothers at the R&B dress business. Hyman Laufer's father worked with them, too. Many Jewish merchants from East Texas bought dresses from them.

I was not the only Jewish lawyer in the area. Herbert Finkelstein was here. Phil Hurwitz came in 1938. Longview's old red brick courthouse had been torn down. The center section of the present courthouse was brand new, and we all thought it was great! I remember a bricklayer telling me that you had to have political input to get a job laying bricks at five dollars a day for the new courthouse. Someone interceded in his behalf so that he could get the work.

I came from Terrell, where we had one of those little Jewish congregations that was familiar to small Texas communities in the early days of the century. It didn't have a name. It was simply the Jewish congregation at Terrell. We didn't have a building, we just met at one place and then another to pray. It was different from the large organizations we know now because we never spent a cent to become members or to participate. We simply had the Jewish congregation at Terrell, and when it declined we didn't have it anymore.

Two of the Torah scrolls in the Longview Temple came from our congregation in Terrell. When the Longview congregation separated from Kilgore, we needed Torahs. The people of Terrell agreed to let us have theirs on the consideration that the Terrell Memorial List would always be read during the memorial service at Yom Kippur.

Several Jewish people lived here before the boom, but there was no organized Jewish congregation like they had in Tyler and Marshall. I remember my grandparents talking about having lived in Tyler when they were young, and enjoying the Jewish community there.

Louis Ritchkie, the tailor, made clothes for gentlemen long before the oil boom. He continued in that business on Fredonia Street. Mayor G. A. Bodenheim was here long before the boom. He was most generous in his contributions to both the Jewish and Christian people. You might say he just believed in religion in general. Bodie was a good businessman and a public relations expert. And he knew how to play politics. "Colonel" Bodenheim was responsible for these brick streets we have in the business district of Longview. The mud in the Kilgore streets was horrible during the boom. It was very different from the situation in Longview, where our wood-block streets had been replaced with those fine bricks.

Jewish people came to East Texas for the same reasons other people came. It was a desperate time, but you could find work and earn a living here. The rest of the country was going through a terrible depression, but because of the oil boom, we were doing well.

CHAPTER 7

Adele Daiches

"Every place you looked in Kilgore there was an oil well pumping. It didn't bother you in the daytime, but at night when everything was still, you would really hear the noise."

The Great Depression brought people from all over the country flocking into Kilgore. The boom happened virtually overnight. One day there were a only few hundred people in Kilgore; the next day there were thousands, and many of them were Jewish. Although some of the Jews who came here went into the oil business and oil-related fields, many Jewish merchants established stores where the oilfield workers could buy the things they needed to make their lives more bearable. Stores stayed open from early in the morning until late at night because the oilfield men worked in shifts.

Most oilfield workers didn't trust the banks. They brought their checks to the Jewish merchants so they could cash them on payday. Oilfield workers were paid much better than the normal income for that day and time. The merchants became acquainted with the men, and they were not the least concerned about cashing their checks. Although there was a lot of cash on hand, it was rare to hear of a robbery or break-in.

My sister Sarah was a young bride when she and her husband, Edward Pfeffer, opened a men's clothing store in Kilgore. She be-

Oil wells in Kilgore, Texas.
—Old postcard in collection of Jan Statman

came ill and had to have a tonsillectomy. There was no hospital in Kilgore, so she was obliged to go home to Pine Bluff, Arkansas, to have the surgery. When she was ready to return to Texas, my mama felt that she was not strong enough to be alone and decided that I should come along to take care of her. I was eighteen years old. You have to remember that it was a different time. In those days, a girl of eighteen was completely innocent. Kilgore was truly an eye-opener for me.

When we stepped off the train at the Kilgore station, we saw men swarming like ants in the streets. They were mostly oilfield workers, but there were con men and other rough people, too. The streets were covered with mud. Dust, when it wasn't mud. You had a choice, dust or mud. In spite of that, it was alive and interesting, except for the mud.

Sarah and Edward's store was at one end of the street, and the only drugstore in town was at the other end. If my sister and I walked to the drugstore to get a Coca-Cola, we heard more curse words than I'd ever heard in my entire life. In fact, I didn't recognize a great many of them.

The six single young Jewish men in Kilgore soon discovered that a Jewish girl had come into town. They had not seen a Jewish girl in many months, and they were eager to meet me. You can imagine what an ego builder it was for me to have all those nice young men treating me like the belle of the ball. One by one, they came to ask my sister for permission to take me out. Sarah and Edward were not much older than I was, but they felt responsible for me. They decided I should not go out with just one of the young men. Since there was safety in numbers, they said all six could take me out together.

And where did they take me but to Mattie's Ballroom! This absolutely innocent eighteen-year-old Jewish girl from Pine Bluff, Arkansas, went to Mattie's Ballroom with six men. We had a wonderful time . . . At least I had a wonderful time!

You behaved yourself when you were at Mattie's. I have heard people say Mattie was her own "bouncer," and I'm sure she could have done it if she wanted to, but she had a great big strong bouncer, and if you didn't behave, he bounced you right out of there.

The best bands in the country came to play at Mattie's, and the dancing was wonderful. You didn't drink in Mattie's during Prohibition. Even if you brought your own bottle, you couldn't bring it into the ballroom; you had to go outside and drink it in your car. There was no cussing, no spitting, no rough behavior of any kind. It was prim and proper, or as prim and proper as a ballroom full of taxi-dancers and oilfield workers could be.

Times were hard in the rest of the country. The depression hurt many people. I had just graduated from high school and my father, who worked hard all his life, found that he couldn't afford to send me to college. I convinced my parents it would be proper and acceptable for me to stay in East Texas, and they reluctantly agreed.

I had to find something to do. Joe Riff and his partner, Mr. Packman, had opened the Palais Royal, a ladies' ready-to-wear shop in Longview in 1931. By the time I arrived, Mr. Riff had bought out Mr. Packman. I walked into his shop, eighteen years old, wanting a job. I told him I had LOTS of experience. The sum total of my experience was that I worked a few Saturday afternoons in somebody's store back home in Pine Bluff. Later on, he teased me about my "lots of experience." But he gave me a chance. I had sold myself in that interview, and that's why he was convinced I would be able to sell to others.

I acquired a rather interesting specialty clientele. I think it was because I was so naive and sincere, but the town's "ladies of the evening" always wanted me to wait on them, and there were plenty of them! Joe Riff had a fine store with lovely merchandise. The most elegant ladies in East Texas shopped there, but without those other special "ladies," he would have had far less business in the early days.

Sometimes the phone would ring and it would be one of my "ladies." She would be in a hotel room with a man who was a liberal spender. She wanted some clothes brought up so that he could buy them for her. Mr. Riff would say, "Oh, no! You are not going to go up there. You pick them out and I'll take them to her."

A nice Jewish girl shouldn't be left alone in the world, so Mr. Riff took it upon himself to be my chaperone. It was the only responsible thing a decent Jewish man could do. Before I could go out on a date, the young man had to check with Mr. Riff. If Mr. Riff said no, I wouldn't go. He was even more protective than my sister and brother-in-law had been.

It was difficult to find a place to live. Sarah and my brother-in-law had a room in one of the big old homes in Kilgore. The lady who owned the home gave them her bedroom, and she moved into another room. There was no place in the house for me to stay, but the house had an attic. They made a bedroom out of it, and I stayed up in the attic. It was hot, but I was young, so the heat didn't bother me. The oil well did.

There was an oil well pumping right outside my window. It was a long time before I was able to sleep with that noise going on. Every place you looked in Kilgore there was an oil well pumping. It didn't bother you too much in the daytime, but at night when everything was still, you would really hear the noise. There's no other sound quite like it in the world. I finally got used to that sound, and after I got used to it I discovered that it would put me to sleep rather than keep me awake.

When I went to work for Mr. Riff, I came out of the attic and moved to Longview. Mr. Riff helped me find a nice room in someone's home. It was much more comfortable than living in an attic.

Finally, after much time and effort, my sister and brother-in-law were able to find a small apartment. Sarah's next-door neighbors, the Seikans, had a little boy. Sarah enjoyed Eva Seikan's little boy so much she decided she had to have a baby of her own. Her daughter, Barbara Ann Pfeffer, was the first little Jewish girl to be born in Kilgore. She was born in Dr. Adams's hospital.

Dr. Adams was a marvelous old family doctor who had his hospital above the drugstore. In those days when you had a baby, you stayed in the hospital for two weeks and when you came home you stayed in the house for four weeks. Dr. Adams said, "It takes you nine months before your baby is born, and you can't get over it in three days." He was kind, caring, knowledgeable, down-to-earth, and he took wonderful care of her.

About three years had passed since my eighteenth birthday, and I had gone home to Arkansas, but when Barbara Ann was born I returned to Kilgore to help my sister.

By this time there was a lot of building going on. Beautiful new churches were being built. My sister continued to be a dear, close friend to the woman who owned the home in which we had lived. The woman had an elderly mother who was devoutly religious. Her congregation built a beautiful church just one block from their house. She sat there, day after day, and watched as they put in every brick of her beautiful new church.

This lovely woman had a grandson who was a bit of a man-about-town. She would often tell me how much it troubled her that her grandson never went to church. I knew the young man. We never dated, of course, but we were friends. One day I said, "Why don't you show me the inside of that beautiful church of yours?" He said, "All right, I will," and we went to the services together. Bless her heart, his grandmother said she watched to see that the roof wouldn't fall in when he walked into the church!

It was during this time that a group of Jewish ladies decided to form a Sisterhood. The Sisterhood came before the Temple. The men got together for minyans in different people's stores here and there, but there was no formal Synagogue or Temple. Our purpose in forming the Sisterhood was to stimulate interest in building a real Synagogue. We called the men together, and they told us that if we would raise fifteen hundred dollars they would somehow manage the rest. That seemed like an impossible sum of money, but we were determined to do it.

I don't know how the idea came to me, but I thought we should have a baby contest. It would not be a pretty baby contest, but a contest to select the healthiest baby in town. The prettiest baby was a matter of opinion, but the healthiest baby was something else again altogether. Of course, when I suggested the idea I was appointed as a committee of one to see about it.

I went to the Kilgore newspaper and asked the advertising man to give me a two-page sketch. The cost was fairly minimal, as it was for charity. I asked him to mark the page off so that I could sell those two pages for a thousand dollars.

He said, "Lady, if you can sell those pages for a thousand dollars, you can have the best job on this newspaper."

We went to all the oil companies, the oil equipment companies, the stores, movie houses. We sold fifty-dollar, twenty-five-dollar, ten-dollar, and five-dollar ads. We sold every bit of it.

Several merchants provided lovely gifts, and the banks opened a little savings account for the winner. By this time there were several doctors in town, and the doctors all cooperated with us. They examined the babies and did the judging. As an added benefit of the contest, many little oilfield babies who might never have had health care had the opportunity to be checked by a doctor. I don't know how many health problems were found and corrected.

It was amazing how many people entered. You won't believe this,

but my sister's little girl won! Of course, we would not give the prize
to her. We didn't think it would be right, partly because she was a
member of the Jewish congregation-to-be, and partly because I was
the head of the contest and she was my niece. It simply would not do.
We selected another baby, even though we all knew that it was our little Barbara Ann who really won. It proved to be a successful community project. We developed a lot of good will, and we presented
the men with fifteen hundred dollars. They managed to raise the rest
of the money, and Temple Shalom was built.

By the time it was completed, I had married and moved to
Gladewater, and from Gladewater to Gilmer. We bought a little shop
in Gilmer and continued to attend services in Kilgore when the meager roads were passable.

We were scrimping and saving in Gilmer, counting coppers to
make them grow when, as it happened, Yom Kippur came on a
Saturday. Gilmer was a farming town. Farmers came into town to do
business on Saturdays. If you didn't do business on Saturday in the
fall of the year, you didn't do business at all. But I felt that Yom
Kippur is Yom Kippur and I put a sign up saying that said, "Closed
for our religious holiday. Open at six o'clock."

The other Jewish merchants in town did not choose to close.
That was their decision. I cannot be critical of them for doing what
they thought they had to do, but our decision was to attend religious
services in Kilgore.

When we returned from Kilgore at six o'clock in the evening, I saw
a tremendous crowd standing outside our store. At first I thought
something terrible had happened, a fire or a robbery. But when we
opened the doors we were swamped! We had the biggest day that we
had ever had in all the time we were in Gilmer. Each person who came
through the doors told me, "We don't have a Christian in this town
who would close his store on a Saturday in the fall of the year for God.
If you can do that, we can wait to spend our money with you."

Isn't that beautiful? People who don't observe their religious holidays are making a terrible mistake. You only get respect if you earn
it. You must respect yourself before you can expect others to respect
you.

The only place to eat out in Gilmer was at a boarding house.
We'd go there every Sunday evening. One Sunday evening there was
a stranger in town. This was most unusual, because we didn't often

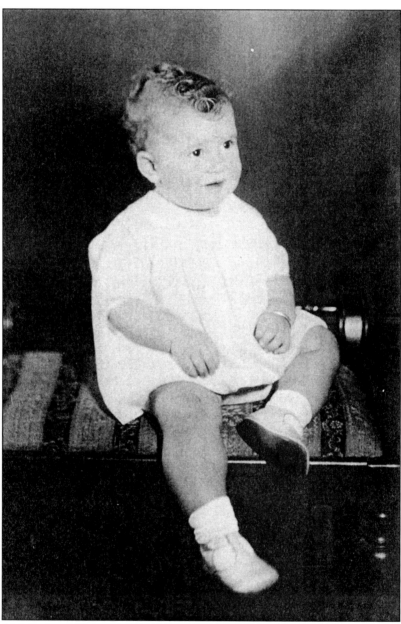

Little Barbara Pfeffer was the "Healthiest Baby" in Kilgore, Texas. Although she won the contest, she was not awarded the prize, because the ladies awarded the prize to someone outside their group.

—Photo courtesy Mike and Gina Joseph

see strangers. In the course of conversation the stranger started saying awful things about the Jews. He lambasted us from Hell to breakfast! I was sitting there growing angrier and angrier.

When he finished I said, "Pardon me, sir, but I happen to be Jewish. You have talked to these good people, and now I am going to tell them the truth."

With that he shoved his chair away from the table and shouted, "I won't sit at the table with a Jewess!"

Two big farm boys happened to be seated at either side of him. When he stood up, they stood up. They each took hold of his shoulders and shoved him back down. They said, "She listened to you, Goddamit! Now you're going to listen to her."

Before I could get down to my shop on Monday morning, the preachers of the community were there. Each one invited me to come and share his pulpit and tell their congregations exactly what I had told that man.

You don't run into that sort of situation often here in East Texas, but that was during World War II. The editor of the Gilmer newspaper later called to tell me that stranger was discovered to be a Nazi who was sent here to incite trouble. He thought Gilmer would be a great place to spread his poison, because he thought the farming people here were stupid and he thought there were no Jews living here. Well, farming people are not stupid, and he met the one person who could show him up for what he was. The good Christian people of Gilmer were good Americans who would not sit still and listen to such filth.

My marriage didn't work out. We had no children, so we agreed to disagree and go our separate ways. I moved away from East Texas. My sister and her husband moved back to Pine Bluff, but they always kept in touch with their friends in Kilgore.

I had known Max Daiches and his brother Fred when I lived in Kilgore. Max was a good friend, and my niece Barbara always called him "Uncle Max." During World War II, like many of the young men in East Texas, Max and his brother went to war. My sister started to write to them because she wanted them to receive as much mail from home as possible. She thought a lot of Max, and all I ever heard from her was "Max this or Max that." Finally, I told her that even though I had been divorced for a long time, I was not interested in Max. Still, she was relentless.

I moved to Kansas City. Eventually, the war was over and the men came home. One evening, my sister and her husband were having dinner at the Adolphus Hotel in Dallas, and who should they meet but Max Daiches. The first thing he did was to ask about me.

"Is she married?"

My sister said no.

His second question was, "What does she look like?"

"She still looks just like me," she told him.

He said, "The next time she is in this area, if you don't call me, I will never speak to you again."

The following summer, my sister and brother-in-law and I were all in Shreveport, Louisiana. Shreveport is close to Kilgore, and it was the only place in the area where you could have a cocktail. We were having cocktails when my sister suddenly snapped her fingers and said, "Oh, my God! I told Max that if you were ever in this area I would call him. Do you mind?"

I said, "I don't care. If you want to call him, call him."

It was exactly five o'clock when she called. He said, "I'll be right there, but in the meantime I want to speak with Adele."

We spoke and I told him, "You'd better hurry or the rest of us will be way ahead of you." That was big talk for me since I take one drink and that's quite enough, but this seemed to be an occasion for big talk.

He said, "That's all right. I'll catch up."

He made the trip from Kilgore to Shreveport in record time. We all went out for a very lovely evening and Max did catch up. In fact, he had a few more of those cocktails than was prudent. My sister suggested it would be a good idea for him to spend the night in Shreveport and return to Kilgore in the morning. He agreed that she was right and he would stay. Then he turned and proposed to me. Just like that!"

I said, "Are you crazy?"

But he meant it. He came to Kansas City to see me several times, but it's difficult to maintain a long-distance relationship. I was convinced that was the end of it when something happened that showed me what I was meant to do.

I was quite successful in my profession. I was a buyer of coats and suits for a large firm, and I was making a lot of money. It was particularly good money for a woman because there were no equal rights then and there was a terrible imbalance in what women and men were paid for the same work. My abilities and my reputation were such that other firms were always offering me better opportunities and even more money.

A Chicago company called me and I flew to Chicago to speak with them. I had good friends in Chicago. If nothing came of the job offer, at least I had the opportunity to visit my friends.

By the time I left Chicago I was very interested in the prospects of the new job. The weather was so bad that the airport was nearly empty. In fact, I realized the only other person on the plane was a priest. We had flown only a few miles when the hostess came out and asked where I was going. I told her I was going to Kansas City and she smiled politely and went away. In a few minutes, here came the pilot.

"Miss," he said, "I'm sorry but we are not stopping in Kansas City. It's fogged in and we are going straight on to San Francisco."

I said, "We're only a few minutes out of Chicago. Turn the plane around and take me back."

He said, "We can't do that either because Chicago was fogging in and it's too dangerous. We can't land in Chicago anymore."

So I sat back and said, "God give me the strength to accept the things I cannot change." I said it out loud and then I said, "If I get fired from my job, I'm going to love working for TWA in San Francisco."

The priest heard this and he came over and said, "Young lady, I heard what you said, and I promise you with that kind of thinking everything is going to be all right. Once you decide what you really want in your life you will get it."

I don't sleep well on planes, so I had nothing to do but think. I asked myself what I really wanted in my life. Did I want this job in Chicago? I was already working too hard. If I worked as hard trying to find a good man, I might find the happiness that had eluded me. I decided not to take the job.

When I finally got home I learned that a friend needed my help in Dallas, so I went to Dallas to help her. She dropped Max a card to tell him I was there. He called the day he got the card and came to Dallas the following evening. He was earnest, but he was a little frightened. He didn't want to ask me to marry him again because he was afraid I would refuse again. Nobody likes to be turned down, and certainly nobody likes to be turned down twice. He came to see me every weekend and we had the opportunity to get to know each other very well, but he didn't ask me to marry him.

I made up my mind that I wanted to marry him, but he was getting entirely too comfortable with the way things were. I told him I was going to take the job in Kansas City.

He said, "I don't want you to go away to Kansas City. You can get a job in Dallas."

I said, "Of course I can, but I won't be paid what I'm worth. If you want to keep me here, put a ring on my finger."

When he returned the following weekend, he not only had a beautiful engagement ring but he had the wedding ring as well. He never asked me to marry him. I asked him. And I never regretted it, because we had a wonderful life together.

We've come a long way since the wide-eyed eighteen-year-old stepped off the train into a Kilgore street filled with dust and mud. East Texas has changed in many ways, and it has remained the same in many ways. It was exciting back then, and it's been exciting ever since.

CHAPTER 8

Al Davis

"The rigs in Kilgore looked like cornstalks growing in a field."

If you ever saw the Spencer Tracy movie *Boomtown*, you'll have a good idea of what an oilfield town was like, muddy streets, rough people, and all. In spite of that image, the oilfield was a great place to be. People came to the East Texas Oilfield from all over the world because anybody who wanted to work could get work here at a time when there were no jobs to be found anywhere else. I can't think of a circumstance where an able-bodied man couldn't find a job. It was hard work, but it was exciting. We didn't suffer the poverty that was prevalent in other parts of the country during the Great Depression.

My family came into the oilfield in a roundabout way. The first family member to come to the United States in 1895 followed the railroad the way my father later followed the oil booms. My father's uncle was a big, tall, strapping man. He couldn't speak a word of English, but like many immigrants, he found a job working on a section gang for the railroad. After a week, the men lined up to be paid $5 for their week's labor. When my uncle reached the front of the line, the paymaster wanted to know his name, but Uncle John couldn't answer because he didn't understand what the man was asking. He was holding up the line. Finally, the paymaster said, "Oh, to hell with it! Your name is John Davis! Put your X right here." He

This view of Main Street in Gladewater, Texas, was taken in the early 1930s. A ring of oil derricks surrounds the town.

—Photo from the collection of Jan Statman

handed him $5 and his name became John Davis. They were willing to pay him to call him John Davis, so he figured that's the way they do things in America. It was okay with him.

The family's name was originally a Slavic derivative of the Yiddish word *shayne*, meaning beautiful, but since Uncle John didn't understand the paymaster in Iowa, and his name became Davis, he told the relatives who followed him, "In America your name is Davis. Don't ask questions. That's the way it has to be." And that's the way it was.

My daddy, E. H. Davis, came to the United States from Prussia in 1906. He went to live with his relatives in St. Joseph, Missouri, and from there he found his way to Texas, where he followed the oil-fields to make a living. My parents started with the Ranger oil boom in 1919. They went on to Cisco, Breckenridge, Burkburnett, Amarillo, Fort Worth, Corsicana. They opened a men's clothing store in Tyler in 1932. It was called E. H. and A. Davis.

My father wasn't a gambler, and he didn't play the stock market. He was not directly in the oil business, but he spent whatever extra little cash he had buying royalties. An oilman friend of his might come in to buy a shirt or a suit and would say, "E. H., I'm going to drill a well and you can have some of the royalties." Dad would say, "Great," and he would buy in.

One interesting aspect of the oil business is the way the oil wells got drilled. Since the East Texas field was a "poor-boy" field, it didn't cost much to drill. The field was so rich and so productive that in the early days if you had a lease you pretty much had a well. The rigs in Kilgore looked like cornstalks growing in a field. The only slight problem was that you had to find the five or ten thousand dollars you needed to drill a well, and nobody had any money.

The driller would take a piece of the action. All he wanted was enough to meet the payroll for his workers. The rest, he would go on. The guy who had the pipe and the drilling rig would take a piece of the action, an eighth interest, a quarter interest, whatever he could negotiate. But no money changed hands. There was no money to change hands.

Most oilfield deals were handshake deals. Hundreds of oil wells were drilled in East Texas on the basis of a handshake in the Gregg Hotel in Longview or the Blackstone Hotel in Tyler. One man might say, "I'll send you a string of pipe. I'll take an eighth interest," and the other man would say, "That's fine." They shook hands and that was that. The only thing people here wanted to know about you was whether you were honest. The oilfield was a small community where everybody knew everybody. You might cheat someone if that's what you wanted to do, but you only did it once and then you'd better be ready to move along, because you weren't going to make it in the oil-field if you had the reputation for being a cheat.

There was a code of honor that was terribly important because everybody in the East Texas field came with the same limited re-sources. This was a poor-boy field. They were all in the same boat. They had to scratch it out in a business that was rounded off to the nearest thousand-dollar bill. The most important thing an oilman had to do was to meet the payroll. After that it was handshakes and buddy-buddy deals. There were a few big guys who stole hundreds of thousands of barrels of oil, but they were already rich and every-body knew about them. For the rest, the code of honor was serious. A man's word was as good as a signed contract. Better! If a man said he was going to do something, you knew he was going to do it.

That's how a lot of the most affluent Jewish families in large cities like Dallas and Houston earned their fortunes. Many of today's largest givers to the United Jewish Appeal and many other worthy Jewish charities in Texas came from that exodus of Oklahoma oilfield equipment people into the East Texas field. They came down from Oklahoma to East Texas with a string of used pipe, and they came up to a man with a lease and negotiated to trade the pipe for part of the well. No money changed hands until after the well was in. If it came in, everybody got rich. If it didn't come in, nothing happened.

The pipe business is a specialized field. They were in the used pipe business, not the junk or scrap business. They were business-men. They were entrepreneurs. They knew how to count. They were willing to take a chance. And most important, they were reli-able, responsible, and scrupulously honest. If they agreed to deliver a string of pipe to a certain place at a certain time, everyone knew it would be there. If they said it was class A or class B or class C pipe, it was. You could believe what they said. They didn't have much money, but they had a few strings of old used pipe left over from the Oklahoma oilfield.

The people in Tyler who really made fortunes in the oil boom were the lawyers. Every one of these deeds to land belonged to insiders and outsiders and somebody who had forty acres of land right after the Civil War but couldn't write and had a hundred fifty heirs all over the place. The lawyers made their money locating those heirs.

Getting a permit to dig a well was another big business which made law firms in Austin rich. You got a permit to drill a well from the Texas Railroad Commission. Theoretically, the permit didn't cost anything, but employing a well-positioned attorney to file your application and pursue it with the Railroad Commission cost quite a lot. I'm not talking about bribes, of course. These were "gentlemanly arrangements." Those gentlemen would make the proper contributions to the proper campaign pledges in the proper names, and that's the way the wells got drilled.

They were producing so much oil in East Texas, it drove the price down. You could buy water for fifty cents a barrel. Oil was only ten cents a barrel. Something had to be done. The State of Texas decided to prorate oil. Proration would limit the amount of oil produced by each well. They passed state regulations, but nobody could enforce them.

The oil producers hated having limits to how much they could produce. The Railroad Commission inspectors were probably only earning $300 a month. The oil producers soon set a price of $300 to pay the inspectors. After they paid that little extra "business expense" they had no more problems with proration! It wasn't legal or legitimate, but to be fair, the inspectors were only human. They could double their income each time they "failed to see" a well that was pumping. Enforcement was so lax it was almost nonexistent.

The governor called in the National Guard, but even they couldn't stop the flow of hot oil. Hot oil runners invented all kinds of clever ways to confuse and confound the enforcers of the law. There were left-handed valves, there were dummy wells, and there was a system called the "bypass."

A bypass would be applied in this way: Suppose I have a lease, and you have a lease right next to mine. We've both got production, and there's one pipeline that's going to handle both our leases. The pipeline comes across your property to mine and then goes on to the next lease. Now, during a nighttime shift, if I hook into the oil that comes from your well, I block the passage of your well into the pipeline and I let it run through my end of the pipeline, and I get credit for the oil which was produced from your lease.

In some quarters that would be called stealing, but in the East Texas oilfield it was called a "bypass." It could be done very inexpensively. It was very illegal, and you could go real far into the jail if you got caught at it, but an awful lot of people made an awful lot of money running hot oil and getting away with it. Slant holes came along later and were far more expensive to accomplish, although they were no less lucrative.

At ten cents a barrel, the world oil market was flooded. East Texas was wrecking the oil industry. Since the State's attempts at proration didn't work, along came Senator Connolly, a powerful man in the national Senate. He teamed up with a fellow named Smith so that we got the Smith-Connolly Act, which made it a federal offense to transport oil across state lines if the oil was in excess of any state's prorations. They couldn't just do it for Texas alone. They had to do it for all the states in the nation. This was a federal law, and it was enforced by the federal marshall. We're talking about serious law enforcement now. You flaunted that law and you'd go to jail. That law cured the overproduction of the East Texas oilfield overnight. The price of oil went from ten cents to seventy cents a barrel and it became stable.

Even after federal proration there were adventuresome people who continued to run hot oil in all kinds of devious ways and by various illegal means. If the oil didn't have to go into interstate commerce, or if it didn't cross the state line, the federal agents couldn't touch it. There were dozens of little independent local refineries in East Texas which could take Citizen A's oil produced in excess of the proration and mix it with Citizen B's oil produced legally and it all got lost in the shuffle. Nobody could tell which was which or where it came from. When it came out of the refinery as gasoline, it could be sold just like anything else. You could get rich if you knew the right people or owned a piece of a semi-illegal little refinery such as that.

I can't think of any Jewish people who were involved with this dark side of the oil business. Most of them were not producers. They were interested in the property as an investment, the way people buy stocks these days. In East Texas during the boom, bringing in a well was a gut cinch. There was little question about whether you were going to get your money back. The question was what the price of oil would be when your well came in.

A few investors, like Izzy Maritsky and his brother, started by buying royalties like my dad did, but they went on to drill wells and had a lot of oil properties. Most of those who actually became oil operators were people in the pipe business who ended up owning interest in so many wells they had to get into producing to protect their investments.

Tyler was a much older, more conservative community than Longview. It was a division point for the Cotton Belt Railroad when cotton was king in Texas and the railroad was important to transporting that cotton. Tyler was a city of about thirty-five thousand people, with about one hundred fifty Jewish families. The Tyler Jewish community was established long before World War I and was thoroughly integrated into the life of the city.

When we came to Tyler, my parents joined the Reform Congregation. The Temple was a well-established institution, and Rabbi Faber was a dignified and impressive man. Some people felt that after they had accumulated capital in the boomtowns they wanted to live a more stable life, so they would move their families to Tyler and commute between the towns.

It is interesting how few members of the established Jewish community of Tyler became involved in the oil business. One reason was that the oil business was considered a little bit "low class." Oil was something of a gambler's profession. They considered many of the people it attracted were not terribly "nice." When your family had been in East Texas for three or four generations, as many of the old-time Tyler Jewish residents had, you viewed oilfield newcomers as interlopers.

Even so, the Jewish people of Tyler were quite hospitable to those of us who moved there. My family lived in a nice house in a nice neighborhood. I graduated from Tyler High School and attended Tyler Junior College, and we had a wonderful time.

By contrast, there were only about a half-dozen Jewish people in Gregg County in 1929, but by 1936 there was an established community and a Temple there as well. Longview was also an established town and railroad center, but it was closer to the oilfield, so that it was simply overrun by oilfield workers. There was production all around Longview, while there was no production close to Tyler. If you lived in Tyler, you had to drive to Gladewater before you got into the oilfield itself. Gladewater and Kilgore were a muddy mess. The dirt roads leading out to the wells would only be graveled when money started to flow, so that they were terribly muddy while the drilling was going on.

A year after we moved to Tyler, my family went into business with the Maritsky brothers in the Davis and Maritsky Men's Clothing Store in Longview. It was a little store, fifteen or twenty feet wide. It had a high ceiling and one of those "airplane" fans that were so loud you couldn't hear yourself think. They stirred up the warm air so that we thought we were comfortable.

My brother Jay Davis came to Longview to help run the store. When I was in high school, I came to Longview every Friday night to help my brother. We opened the store at 7:30 in the morning and stayed until customers stopped coming in late at night. Then we went to Mattie's Ballroom to dance all night.

I was a high school kid and I lived with my parents in Tyler all week, but I lived with my brother in his garage apartment on my "wild" Longview weekends. I lived in two different worlds, and it was interesting to go from one world to the other.

During the boom times, the people who came into the oilfield were interested in drilling wells and making money, and they didn't care what you were as long as you were honest and did what you said you were going to do.

Oh, you might hear comments about the "Jew merchant," or "Jewing" with you when they wanted to bargain, but that was only what they used to hear back in Pennsylvania or Oklahoma, or wherever they came from. They didn't even know that what they were saying was offensive. It was said without malice and was usually interpreted the way it was said.

Growing up in the oilfields gave us freedom that's hard for people in larger cities to imagine. We grew up without the kind of structure that caused people to worry about what other people thought about them because they were Jewish. Everybody knew we were Jewish. I didn't even know it could be a problem. In many established cities, the "five o'clock rule" still holds. If you've never heard about the "five o'clock rule," it's simply this: You do business with people, you work with them, you socialize with them at lunch. You're all close friends until five o'clock. At five o'clock the Christians go their way and the Jews go theirs. There is little social interaction.

This silly situation didn't exist in our oilfield towns. We lived in a free and open society where your friends were your friends before and after five o'clock. It was a great place to grow up. You could do anything you were capable of doing, socially or in business. Any Jewish person or family who wanted to become involved in social or civic activities in the East Texas communities was welcome to do so, and a great many did and still do.

Of course you didn't go to work for the major oil companies. Those decisions were made in big eastern cities where things were quite different. But people here in East Texas weren't all that concerned about the major oil companies, because the majors didn't control this field. The independent poor-boy East Texas oil companies were never that shortsighted. They needed good, hard-working people. If you could work hard enough to earn your pay, you were welcome.

Even though we all worked hard, young people could find a lot to do for entertainment. Mostly we went to dances. If you couldn't dance, you weren't going to have a good time, but somebody would soon take you aside and teach you how to dance. We had all the big bands come and play for us. Tommy Dorsey, Benny Goodman, and bands of that quality were eager to come here. Not just to Mattie's Ballroom, but to other East Texas places, as well. They knew they would have good audiences, and they knew there was money here so they were sure to be paid.

In Tyler on Saturday nights, we had a dance that cost one dollar. That was per couple, not per person. We danced the two-step, the foxtrot and the East Texas flea hop. If there wasn't a dance, we would meet at the Tyler Women's Club and play their nickelodeon, or go to somebody's house and dance to the music of a phonograph. It was not wicked at all. Of course we had our bad kids like any other society has, but they were ostracized. We didn't have time for them. We were having too much fun.

The older generation, the families with kids, people like my parents, quickly developed Jewish communities with all the same characteristics of any Jewish community in any other small southern town. The only difference was that because of the opportunities that were available, their hard work allowed most of them to prosper.

One sure way to find out where the Jewish people were was to follow the "Schnorrers," the beggars, the professional fundraisers for small religious charities, as they made their way across the state. Texas

was a big territory for the guys with the long black coats and the ritual fringes. They swarmed into East Texas in the 1930s like black-
coated locusts. They heard there was money here, and they wanted
some of it. When they came into our store my dad always gave them
a contribution. I would say, "Who was that, Dad? What did he want?"

"He wanted two dollars," my dad would tell me.

"Why did he want two dollars?"

"For charity."

"What charity?"

"Jewish charity."

"Did you give him two dollars?"

"Of course I gave him two dollars."

It bothered me to see my father give his hard-earned money to
someone who did not make it clear where the money was going. I'd
say, "Daddy, what's he going to do with that money?"

"It's for a Jewish cause," my father would tell me.

"Which Jewish cause?"

"He came from such-and-such a Jewish organization."

"Did anybody check and see if there really is such an organization?"

"Never mind. The man needed money and I gave it to him," my
daddy would say. "I'm thankful I'm able to be the one who can give
instead of the one who has to ask."

I'm sure some of the causes were legitimate. I'm sure some were
not, but when the Jewish community members contributed to the
Schnorrers they felt they were doing something to help the greater
cause of Judaism. And if that's not exactly where the money went, at
least they knew they were helping another human being.

After the first rough years of the boom, the drifters moved on
down the road to the next oilfield and the next boomtown, but the
Jewish people of the oilfield stayed. We helped build hospitals and
schools, symphonies and libraries. We paved the roads and settled
down to become an important part of our new hometowns.

CHAPTER 9

Irving Falk

"I didn't know whether to look up, down, sideways, or look out for traffic."

My first visit to Kilgore at the age of eighteen put me in complete awe. Downtown Kilgore was nothing but a narrow passage through the mud, with two-way traffic, trucks, and everybody double-parked in the crowded streets. If you were on foot, you tried to stay on the wooden pavement, because when you got off the pavement there was nothing but mud and dirt and oil-contaminated mess. I didn't know whether to look up, down, sideways, or look out for traffic. I couldn't imagine how the city could exist with that much oil in it. The oil wells looked like a dense forest. Oil derricks as far as you could see!

I arrived in June when it was hot. By September and October it started to rain. It didn't stop. It rained for forty days and forty nights. You'd see teams of mules pulling trucks, trying to get them out where they'd been stuck down to the hubs of their wheels in mud.

The roads were only navigable when it was dry, but it was never dry, so that the roads were never navigable. If you had a truck you'd have to get teamsters who had teams of six or twelve mules to pull your truck through the bad areas out to where your well might be. My oldest brother, Louis, came to Shreveport in 1926 to visit our uncle, Izzie Gelfand. While he was there, Louis became friendly with some people in the oil business, and Uncle Izzie invited him to stay. In the early 1930s this East Texas oilfield came in and created great opportunities for people who were willing to work. No one could believe there could be so much oil in one oilfield. There had never been a field this large, or having this much production.

Louis came back to New Jersey to visit the family and talked me into leaving school and coming here to work with the new oilfield in Texas. I knew nothing about oilfields, but I came along. I was a shy and frightened kid, just off the farm. I was in a shell and had to come out of that shell in a hurry. I had no idea of what Texas would be like. It was an adventure.

By this time, my brother was in business in Monroe, Louisiana, and also in Shreveport. He had an interest in a plant in El Dorado, Arkansas, which was an old, worn-out oilfield. The El Dorado field was about twenty to twenty-five years old and had depleted itself in a short time. Louis sent me to El Dorado to visit with some people he knew. They gave me my first glimpse of an oilfield. When I got there they were "pulling the field," taking it apart by recovering the pipe that was put down in the wells.

After I learned what I could learn in El Dorado, he decided it was time for me to come to Texas. I came here and met Sam Weldman. Sam was thirty-five or thirty-six years old. I was eighteen. I looked up to him and he became sort of a father image to me. I never would have made it without him.

We made an interesting combination, Sam was the "inside man" and I was the "outside man." You can imagine me, at eighteen, being the "outside man," going around the countryside looking for pipe and scrap iron and salvageable items that could be reconditioned and sold to the people who were developing this oilfield.

I called on oil companies who had salvage yards within their oil camps and I would buy used pipe. If it had no further use as pipe, we would cut it up and make scrap iron out of it. It took all my courage. I was very shy and frightened. When people would ask me how old I was, I would tell them I was twenty-one. That sounded sophisticated to someone who was eighteen, and it gave me a bit of courage. I don't know whether they believed me or not, but they acted as though they did.

One of the first things I tried to do when I came here was to adopt a Texas accent, because I thought it was attractive. I liked it, and people here liked to hear me do that. At least I was trying to fit in. I'd say, "yes, sir, and yes, ma'am, and y'all come back." It was a pleasant way of speaking. I was young enough to adapt, and before I knew it, I was speaking pretty much like everybody else.

There weren't many Jewish people my age. We didn't even have a Temple when I came here. A little later they built the synagogue in Kilgore. I would go there for the High Holy Days, but most of the time I'd go to Shreveport to be with the family.

I was a stranger in a wild place. At first, I was not all that welcome by the Longview people, because they were trying to protect themselves and their families from the riff-raff that the oil brought in. They were suspicious of strangers. Every train that came into Longview had all kinds of desperate people on it. Until they got to know you, and know that you were a serious person and were here with a business, the local people were suspicious of you. I was a pretty serious person at eighteen. I eventually met some people who would accept me for who I was and I made some friends.

Young people can always find something to do for fun. I spent my time with an occasional date, reading a book, watching picture shows, and taking trips to Shreveport to visit my family. There were probably a half-dozen movie theaters in Longview. Baseball was a big thing here, too. We had minor league baseball teams. They could play night games because the gas flares lit up the night. There was no difference between day and night in the oilfield. It was always light.

If you were a dancer, there were lots of places to go dancing in this wild and wooly place. If you couldn't get a date, you'd go to Mattie's, where the taxi dancers would dance with you for ten cents a dance. Every place that had a crossroad would have a dozen honkey-tonks, and they would operate around the clock to accommodate the people who worked around the clock on the drilling rigs. They might get off at five o'clock in the morning or two in the afternoon and they would want to go out and have a beer. Day and night meant nothing to them. Some of these beer joints had brothels in the little cabins behind them. A lot of that activity took place outside the city limits. Outside of town there were crossroads where oilfield workers were living in tents. Those tent cities would be called "Camp" this or "Camp" that.

We built a little warehouse and built a little apartment above the warehouse so that I had a place to live. My means of transportation

Oilfield equipment was heavy, rough, and coated with mud.

—Photo from the collection of Jan Statman

was a pickup truck. I used that pickup for everything. I'd haul scrap iron on it, go out on dates in it, and court with it.

I grew up on a dairy farm in Passaic, New Jersey. My parents were originally from Russia. They migrated at the turn of the twentieth century. We had a rustic life on our farm, and it was a hard life. We had cows in the pasture and chickens in the pen. We got up at three o'clock in the morning, milked the cows twice a day, boiled the bottles, bottled and delivered milk, and worked a twenty-four-hour day. We didn't know we were poor. I didn't even know I was working hard. Life on the farm was harder than life in the East Texas oilfield. When I came here, I only worked an eight-hour day, so I thought I was on vacation!

The most astonishing thing to me was that there was so much of everything here. There was a severe depression all over the country. When I left home there were people in New Jersey who couldn't afford to feed their children. Here in East Texas, you saw big flashy diamond rings, and people with silver and gold belt buckles or fancy silver-tipped leather cowboy boots.

What also amazed me was that you would see beautiful brand-new cars parked alongside little rundown, unpainted shacks. The oilfield people had pride in their cars, pride in their boots, pride in their hats, but they didn't seem to care about their houses. It only made sense after it was explained to me. They were only in that house temporarily, but the cars and the boots and the fancy belt buckles would go along with them when they moved on to the next oilfield or the next.

Eventually, we brought our whole family south. Another brother landed in Jackson, Mississippi. My sister Betty was in Texarkana; my sister Fannie and my brother Meyer were in Jackson, Mississippi. When I was called into the service to serve my country in World War II, I brought my sister Ada's husband Morris Milstein to Longview to look after my business. My brother Louis bought a large home in Shreveport and brought my parents to Louisiana.

My parents were Orthodox. They were delighted to have a fine home within walking distance of the Synagogue. On the farm, on the High Holy Days and sometimes even on Shabbat, they would walk four miles to the Synagogue and four miles back.

I've heard many stories about hot oil, that is, illegal oil. I heard many stories of the National Guard and the Texas Rangers arresting people for running hot oil. Some of them might be exaggerated, but most of them are true and then some. There was so much oil taken out of this East Texas field that the price of oil got down to ten cents a barrel. The government decided we were wasting our natural resources and driving the price of oil down, so they passed rules to conserve the oil and stabilize the prices. The Railroad Commission said, "This is what we've got to do. We're going to allow only a limited number of barrels to be taken out of a well in a specified time." Now, you must remember there was an oil well every twenty-five feet inside the city limits of Kilgore. They were so close the derricks were touching one another. There were even more wells all up and down the countryside, so that was still quite a lot of oil being produced.

To be fair, the independent oilmen didn't have any money. They were drilling by the seat of their pants. They borrowed money to drill those wells, and they thought they were going to pay the expense of drilling with fifty-cents-per-barrel oil. But when the price was down to ten cents per barrel, they had to produce five times as much oil in order to achieve the payment they had to make. They may not have wanted to break the rules, but many of them felt they didn't have a choice. It was the only way to survive.

Also, many of these independents figured, "This is my well, I paid for it, I drilled it, it's mine. Why should anybody else tell me what I can or cannot do with it?" So they took the law into their own hands and figured they would decide how much oil they would take out of their own wells. They invented all sorts of clever ways to fool the officials.

Some of the independents who were drilling the wells even decided they didn't want to take a chance with the money they had borrowed. They didn't want to run the risk of drilling a dry hole. It wasn't honest, but they would simply go underground and drill into their neighbor's well, which they knew was already producing.

In addition to that, they could drill wells that were slanted into their own producing wells. The rumor was that every well that was drilled around the perimeter of the East Texas field was slanted. There were like straws going down to one place. There might be one good producing well, but it was only allowed to produce a certain amount of oil each month. The fake, or "dummy," wells were slanted so they were taking oil from the bottom of that one good producing well. Each of these was allowed to produce a certain amount of oil each month, even though they really weren't producing anything at all. That made it possible for the well owner to appear to obey the rules.

I'd have some interesting experiences in the salvage business. I'd have a farmer call on me and ask me if I was interested in buying an oil storage tank. I'd say, "Where did you get an oil storage tank?" He'd say, "Somebody put an oil storage tank on my farm. He hasn't paid rent for two or three years, so I want to sell this tank." It was a hot oil tank that had been hidden down on the bottom area of a farm, been used for a time, and then abandoned.

There was a lot of theft going on. Police protection was crude. If you travel into the oilfield, with its roads leading in different directions, you can see how it would be easy for someone who knew his way around out there to escape when something was stolen.

East Texas has changed. The only industry we knew in the 1930s was the oilfield. When I came here there were a thousand oil wells being drilled. Kilgore alone had a thousand oil wells. Some wells were producing five thousand barrels a day. It was the world's largest oilfield, and there was nothing else like it.

One of the first questions I asked when I came here was, How long will this last? The answer was that it would last approximately thirty years in the middle of the field. That was in 1930, and they're still saying some of the wells will last thirty years. The field has slowed down, but it's still here, and many of the people who came in with the boom are still here, too.

CHAPTER 10

Dan Felsenthal

"He took her out to the field where the ground was rumbling and shaking. They were about to blow a gusher, and he wanted her to see it come in."

When Napoleon's decree called for all Jews to have proper surnames, a man named Isaac was late arriving at the village meeting. He said that he had to travel over "hill and dale" to get there. "Fels und Thal" became the family name.

My grandfather, Sonnel Joseph Felsenthal, was born in El Dorado, Arkansas, in 1900. My grandfather's family had been in the United States since 1854 when three brothers came to Chicago from Alsace Lorraine. One of the brothers, Rabbi Bernhard Felsenthal, was influential in the Reform Movement in the United States. He started the Sinai Congregation in Chicago in 1861 and Temple Zion in Chicago in 1864.

His brother, David Felsenthal, had moved to Camden, Arkansas, and like many families, the brothers found themselves divided by the Civil War. Rabbi Bernhard was a prominent figure in the North and was respected by President Lincoln. His brother David fought with honor for the Confederacy. We can only imagine the hardships of families torn apart by the war. However, when David was taken as a prisoner of war in February 1862, near Springfield, Illinois, his brother Rabbi Bernhard interceded with President Lincoln. David was released almost immediately from the prisoner of war camp. He returned to Camden, Arkansas, and lived out the rest of his years there.

David had nine children. Two of his sons, Isaac and Adolph, were involved in buying and selling property. While the rest of the family remained in Camden, Isaac moved about the state, buying and leasing property. That's why his son Sonnel was born in El Dorado.

When Sonnel grew up, he and his father continued in the business of buying and leasing property. Because of this, they were involved in the Smackover Field oil boom in El Dorado in the early 1920s. When the boom hit in East Texas in 1930, it was quite natural for Sonnel to migrate this way. Through his business of buying and leasing land he became involved in the oil business.

He was one of the few Jewish people who was actively and personallly involved in the oil business. He was a large interest owner in the Willow Springs Field, in the Spring Hill area north of Longview. One of the people he worked with was Sam Dorfman. He had some property close to where the Delta Drilling Company took over and was there in the formative years of the Delta company. His involvement unfolded as the years went on.

My aunt Sherry told the story that one night he came into her bedroom, woke her up, and said, "Come on, Sherry. You have got to see this!" He took her out to the field where the ground was rumbling and shaking. They were about to blow a gusher, and he wanted her to see it come in. It was something she would never forget.

My grandmother, Annette Silverberg Felsenthal, grew up in Shreveport, where her parents, Frank and Rose Silverberg, were jewelers. She met my grandfather by mistake. My grandfather had asked her sister Marie to go out on a date. When he came to call for Marie she was not ready, so he asked my grandmother if she would like to go instead. She said, "Sure," and their romance developed from there. I'm not sure how long they courted, but they were married in 1931, the year the boom hit in Gregg County.

The newlyweds came to Longview, and at first they lived in the Sample Apartments next to the Community Center downtown. Then they built a home in the Mobberly Place Addition. A newspaper article of the time said, "Colonel Felsenthal Building Home in Mobberly Place." I don't know why he was called "Colonel." As far as I know he was never in the service. Maybe it was a nickname? Maybe it was an honorary title?

Like people all over America, my grandmother's parents came upon hard times. The lost their business in the Great Depression. They stayed in Shreveport for a while but eventually moved to Longview, where Sonnel and Annette took care of them financially for the remainder of their lives. Rose Silverberg was a gifted pianist and organist who played for the Methodist church and for many of the Protestant congregations in Longview.

My grandmother Annette was quite social. She often had luncheons or bridge parties and poker parties for the ladies at her house. She was a dedicated and highly awarded bridge player and had a large shelf of trophies. My dad, Daniel Felsenthal, was adopted in 1941. He was born in Shreveport. Dr. Andres helped with his adoption. The custom of the time was for doctors to help match adopting families with healthy babies. Dad's little sister Sherry was adopted in 1948. She came from Edna Gladney in Dallas. It was very important to my grandparents to have children, and they loved them both dearly.

In 1955, my grandparents attended a meeting to plan the construction of the new Temple Emanu-El in Longview. My grandfather pledged to donate the money to construct the social hall. Shortly afterward, he was involved in a horrible traffic accident. He was rushed to the hospital in very bad condition. The nurse came into his room, and, thinking he was asleep, she asked the family what they wanted her to do in case the end came.

"I don't know very much about Jewish people and your customs," she apologized. "I need to know who you would want me to call if his condition should become grave. I know that Catholic people would want me to call the priest and Protestants would want me to call their minister. Who would Jews want me to call?"

My grandfather raised up in bed as best he could and said, "Jews want you to call a doctor!"

Of course the doctor was called, but there was little he could do. My grandfather passed away.

My grandmother honored his wishes and his pledge. The social hall at Temple Emanu-El was built. A plaque in the social hall states that it is the "Felsenthal Hall, in memory of my beloved husband, Sonnel J. Felsenthal, November 8, 1899–January 15, 1955."

CHAPTER 11

Milton Galoob, Sarah Picow, and Celia Bergman

"Our parents were 'boomers.' They followed the boom, opening stores in all the little oilfield boomtowns."

East Texas was a wild place in 1931 when our sister Celia and her husband Dave opened their women's clothing store in Longview. Our brother Milton was seventeen years old when he graduated from high school that year. He was a gifted pianist and had earned a scholarship to the Chicago Conservatory of Music, but the depression made it impossible for him to go to college because even with his scholarship, things were so bad our parents couldn't afford to pay his living expenses.

Our brother Jack Kins had a store in Kilgore. At seventeen, Milton used to haul merchandise back and forth between Kilgore and Oklahoma. It was three hundred fifty miles, all of it rough road, but the road between Gladewater and Kilgore was the worst. It was so bad it would shake the headlights right off his old Ford. He had to have them welded back after every trip!

After Jack went bust in Kilgore, Prohibition was repealed and beer came in. Jack went to work for his brother-in-law, Leon Sollinger, who owned a pool hall in Tyler. Then Leon went bust, so he and Jack started to sell Postal Telegraph clocks. Milton also got a job with the Postal Telegraph Company, selling clocks in Oklahoma. When he couldn't get a down payment, Milton would trade clocks for gas, for beans, for bread, for just about anything. He'd be happy to give the clock away because at the end of the week he got a commission of eight dollars for every clock he sold. He was making seventy or eighty dollars a week. That was big money during the depression! At least it was big money until the company started repossessing the clocks for nonpayment. The company started taking Milton's commissions back, so he quit selling clocks.

When the clocks blew up, Milton came to Longview to live with Celia. He was broke, but he knew Celia would find a way to feed him. Things were so bad by then that he couldn't even afford to buy tires. He drove all the way from Oklahoma to Longview, Texas, on two tires and two rims!

When Prohibition was finally repealed and beer was legalized, Leon Solinger and Jack found Milton a job with Fritz Glazer, who had "The Real Juice Company." That was the bottling name for the beverage wholesaler Glazers. They were in soda pop during Prohibition and got into the beer business when it became legal that summer. Fritz married Margaret Solinger in 1936, and they remained in this area for several years.

Milton started out with his old Model A Ford, selling Union Beer and Schlitz Beer for a dime a case. Gas was eight cents a gallon, which wasn't bad if you had the eight cents. Three months later, he was able to buy a pickup truck. He wasn't handling kegs until Sam "Honey" Donsky taught him how to tap a keg of beer, how to treat his customers well, and everything else he needed to know to be in the business. Honey Donsky was an excellent beer man.

While Honey Donsky was teaching Milton the beer business, the man who had the Stag Bar in Kilgore would sell fifteen to twenty kegs of beer on an average Saturday. There weren't any paved streets in Kilgore, so they would back the truck up as close as they could get, and then they had to roll the kegs through the mud to the bar. Those wooden kegs weighed two hundred thirty pounds each. Milton weighed one hundred forty pounds. The kegs had no handles, and you had to manhandle them, roll them through the mud. They really had to "roll out the barrel"! Sometimes the patrons would come out of the bar to help roll the barrels through the mud.

Milton Galoob at work.

After a year, Milton got the Pabst account and went into business for himself. All he could afford to buy was one pickup truckload of beer at a time. He would drive to Shreveport every other night to get his truckload. Since he had no other place to store it, he left his pickup truck full of beer in Celia's garage.

He would bootleg Jax beer. All the other beers brought a dollar and sixty cents a case, but Jax was a hot number and it brought three dollars a case. Milton had a few customers he would sell Jax for two dollars and fifty cents and save them fifty cents a case. He was making ninety cents a case, which was good money for him and a good deal for them.

Four Jewish brothers, Harry, Joe, Jake, and Morris Schulman, had a barbecue stand in Longview in the early '30s. Their barbecue was so good they got fifteen cents for a sandwich when hamburgers were selling at six for a quarter downtown. They'd buy their beer from Milton. Harry was married to a Christian woman. Jack married Mrs. Miller's daughter Billie. Mrs. Miller owned the New York Dress Store in town and knew absolutely everything that was going on.

When our younger sister, Sarah, graduated from high school, she came to live with Celia. Milton never let Sarah get around the beer business, but she knew everything that was going on because she used to hear him talk about his customers and all the "fine" people he would deal with.

Milton soon became the seventh distributor in the United States to handle canned beer. A carload of beer would come in COD with the bill of lading attached. He had to pay three thousand dollars before he could touch it. He had enough friends in Longview that he could go to them on a Saturday night and borrow the money to get the carload of beer on Monday morning. He always paid them as soon as it was sold.

The Galoobs had a lot of family members here during the oil boom years. "Honey" and Margaret Donsky lived with Mama Galoob for nine months before they moved to Tyler. Jack and Sweetie Kins were in Longview. The Futeranskys had a grocery store next to the Rita Theater on Tyler Street.

Milton married Minnie Balter from Freeedom, Pennsylvania, and there were lots of Balters here, too. From the Balter side of the family, there were Sid and Rae, Ann and Norman, Benjie and Minnie, and Ace and Iris. Cousin Ben Balter was married to Izzie Maritsky's niece Marguerite.

A number of Jewish people lived in the area before the boom. Mr. Richkie, the tailor, was married to a Christian woman and raised their three daughters as Christians, although he always remained a Jew. Old Man Bodenheim was mayor of Longview. Although he married a Christian woman and raised his sons as Christians, Bodie never denied that he was Jewish, and he gave a donation to the Temple every year until he died. He made a nice contribution to help fund one of the Sunday school rooms, too.

The numbers greatly increased after the boom. Ben Scrinovsky had a liquor store in Gladewater. His nephew Bill Scrinovsky had a ready-to-wear store and also a cafe. The Sanovs were in business in Gladewater. Nap and Sally Scher and Leon Gans had a men's clothing store. The Denowitzes had a store called "Carolane's."

Carrie and Joe Riff and a partner named Packman opened the Palais Royal ladies' store in February 1931. Mr. Packman stayed for less than a year. Carrie's sister's son, D. L. Silverman, came to live with them when he was fourteen or fifteen years old. Carrie raised her nephew as though he was her own child. He was a sweet, nice boy. He became a pilot and was the first serviceman from Longview to be killed in World War II. He was killed right after Pearl Harbor.

Sam Dorfman, Dave Eisenberg, Sonnel Felsenthal, and Ike Rudman were all in the oil business. Sam Dorfman owned the Louisiana Pipe and Supply Company. He was also a cofounder of Delta Drilling. The Davis family from Tulsa, Oklahoma, owned the Producers Pipe and Supply Company and employed a number of Jewish men.

Izzy Levinson and his wife Ida were partners in the scrap business with a man whom everybody knew only as Mr. Booken. His wife, of course, was known only as Mrs. Booken. Irving Falk worked with Sam Weldman in the Texas Scrap Material Company. He brought his sister and brother-in-law, Ada and Morris Milstein, here to run the business when he was called away to the service during World War II.

Abe Silverman and his brother Louis opened a shoe store in a location that was vacated by two other Jewish merchants, Scrinopskie and Polsky, in 1934. Abe's brother Jack worked for the Stanolin Oil Company, His parents, Dora and David Silverman, were living here when Abe married Helen on New Year's Eve, 1939. They raised their son Barry and their daughter Lana here.

Manny Franks managed the K. Wolen's store. He and his wife Evelyn had a daughter and son. Louie Bernstein and Bernie Weinstein also worked for the K. Wolens store. Bernie and his wife Ruth came here in 1933. They later had one daughter, Terrie, a darling little blond girl.

Bernard Henry had a store. Ben Scrinovsky opened a men's clothing store in Mr. Richkie's building and he put his nephew Bill in it. Bill was already married to Ytis Rudman, who was the neice of Mrs. Miller of the New York Dress Shop. Jay Davis and Izadore Maritsky had a men's store. Bill Pilon owned a shoe shop. Miss Rosie

Friedlander had a bakery. Sidney Blatt opened a ladies' ready to wear store, even before he married Martha Daiches. They had one daughter, Rowena. His brother Maurice and his wife Molly came to Longview to run the store when Sidney was called away to serve his country during World War II. The Blatts were originally from Canada. Katz and Selliger came from El Dorado, Arkansas, to open the K.C. store. Although Mr. Katz remained a bachelor, Frank Seliger and his wife Hilda had two sons, Maurice and Lewis.

Morris Sosland came to Longview when the boom hit in 1930. He started out with showcases of jewelry in the Longview Drug Store. He later had a beautiful jewelry store with fine crystal and china. He and his wife Etta had two sons, Jay and Leonard. Everybody's loveliest wedding gifts came from their store. Morris Sosland's brother, Abe Sosland, had a jewelry counter in the Crane's Corner Drug Store, which he later moved to a location next to the First National Bank.

During the '30s there were at least seventy-five Jewish families in this area. Like many small southern cities, downtown Longview and downtown Kilgore would shut for the High Holy Days. All the stores would be closed.

Life in Longview during the oil boom was more than work. There was social life as well as a religious life. Before they organized a Temple in Kilgore, the Longview people held High Holiday services in the hall above McCarley's jewelry store. One of the men conducted a simple, straightforward service.

There was a big social life for the younger Jewish people in the area. Cab Calloway, Tommy Dorsey, Benny Goodman, and every other big band in the country played right here in Longview at the original Mattie's Ballroom, which was located between Longview and Kilgore on the old Kilgore Road. It was boiling hot in the summer and freezing cold in the winter, but that didn't matter to anyone.

A boy could take his date to Mattie's, but if he didn't have a date, Mattie had dime-a-dance girls to dance with the oilfield workers. If someone wanted to dance with good dancers, those girls were excellent. Milton learned to dance at a dime-a-dance place in Seminole, Oklahoma. His brother Jack gave the girls fifty tickets—that was five dollars' worth—and said, "Teach the kid to dance." Milton was fourteen years old.

Milton and Sarah also went to Jewish dances in Tyler on Sunday nights where the young, single Tyler, Longview, and Shreveport Jews in their early twenties socialized together. Louie Ettelman and Charlie Cohen held those dances in a big barn. They had two black musicians and a drummer. Young people might not have gone to synagogue because the roads were so bad, but they went to those dances!

With so many young people in town, there were quite a number of romances. Our sister Reva was friendly with Fanye Margulis. Fanye's father, Morris Margulis, and Mama Galoob came from the same town in Russia. For some reason, Mr. Margulis always wore a heavy winter coat, even in the hottest days of the summer. He never took it off. Mr. Margulis, his wife D'voryah, and their children, Melvin, Rose, Sarah, and Fanye, first settled in Mount Pleasant. They moved from Mount Pleasant to Longview in 1935. They were partners with George Levinson of Kilgore in the scrap business. Fanye was a sweet, beautiful girl and a wonderful, devoted daughter.

Reva conspired to make a match between Fanye and the man who would become her husband, Harold Unker. Reva was working at the Harmon General Hospital. Harold was a lonely, unhappy kid from New York City. He hated being here, he hated the food, he hated the heat, he hated Texas, he hated everything. In spite of all this, he was a nice boy, so Reva engineered a way for a friend of his at the hospital, an Italian boy who was also from New York City, to introduce him to Fanye. He told Harold that he'd met a very lovely girl. She was Jewish and he thought Harold should call her. Fanye was so sweet and beautiful, how could Harold help falling in love with her? They were married while he was on leave, in 1944.

Milton's romance with his wife Minnie was something out of a storybook. Minnie's brother, Sid, played football for Centenary College in Shreveport. All his brothers and his sister eventually came to Shreveport to visit him.

Milton stopped at Celia's store every morning before he started his day's rounds. He didn't really stop to socialize. Either he stopped to get money, or to see how short he was at the bank that day. One morning in early October, he was just leaving Celia's store when Ben Balter's wife, Marguerite, pulled up and motioned for him to come over to the car and meet her friend. Milton fell in love with Minnie as soon as he saw her. He had a date with her that very next night.

He took her to Mattie's Ballroom, where he promptly got drunk and proposed to her, right then and there, on the dance floor. She thought he was crazy, but he was determined and he pursued her all the way to Pennsylvania. They were married in Pennsylvania on New Year's Day. He didn't remember much about the wedding. All he knew was that he had never been so cold in his life!

Celia said she was already grown up and married so she didn't have all that much fun because she "came here COD—cash on delivery."

Times weren't always COD for the Galoob family. They worked hard but were extremely comfortable before the depression. They even had a surrey with a fringe on top, just like in the song. The depression changed all that. The depression changed so many lives.

"Our parents never would talk about the life they lived in Europe before they came to America," Celia explained. "America was everything to them. We know that they were poor in the Old Country, although our mother refused to admit it. She would always say, 'We weren't all that poor because we came here with a pierna, a feather mattress.' She was so proud of that thing! It represented something important to her. We kept it for years.

Our father came to America from Lithuania, which was then part of Russia. He was conscripted into the Russian army when he was only fourteen years old, but he ran away to America. When you hear about young Jewish boys who ran away to avoid going into the Russian army, you must understand that going into the Russian army was not like going into the army in this country. It was virtually a death sentence for a Jewish boy. Hardly any of them survived, and those few who did survive never saw their families again.

Our father had a strong will to live. Traveling alone by night, and sleeping in haystacks during the day, this little fourteen-year-old boy, all alone, worked his way across Europe to Germany, where he managed to find steerage passage. His sister Molly and his brothers, Alec and Sam, were already in America, so he knew that if he was able to reach this country, he would survive.

He made it to New York City. He was living with his sister Molly when a cousin in Oklahoma City convinced him to come west, where the opportunities were greater. That's how people survived in those days. One or two members of a family would earn money for passage. They would work and save every penny so they could send for the next one and the next until they had sent for the rest of the family.

The same thing happened in our mother's family. Two of our mother's brothers, Usha and Penni Ammerman, came to America to work and save and send for the others. Uncle Penni came first; then he brought Uncle Usha over. They both found jobs with the Philadelphia Interurban Company. The company didn't allow relatives to work together, so one of them changed his name. That's how they became Spitz and Ammerman. They both worked on the same trolley car. One was a motorman and one was a conductor, and between them they stole enough to bring the other six relatives over, five cents at a time! Our uncles weren't exactly horse thieves, but trolley car thieves are colorful, too. After that, they were both bootleggers in Oklahoma, where they brought their whiskey in by Railway Express.

Our mother, Rebecca Ammerman, came to America in 1895, traveling with our grandfather, Herschel Ammerman, his new wife, a younger sister, and a brother. They came from Kesilla, a little Russian village close to Odessa and Kiev. Our grandmother Sarah had died. Our grandfather married his second wife the week before he left Europe. He also brought a niece, Sophie Futeransky, who was only eighteen months old. Mama was fourteen years old, and she held little Sophie in her arms all the way across the ocean until they arrived at Ellis Island.

Mama grew up and worked hard. She married Sam Kins. They had two children, Celia and Jack, but her husband died very young.

Mama was a widow with two small children, and she wanted to be near her own family. Her brothers had gone west to the Oklahoma Territory, so she decided she would go to the Oklahoma Territory to find them. She packed up her children and got on the train. Oklahoma was a big place, but she somehow managed to find her brothers, and she found she could earn a living for herself and her children by running a store in Oklahoma City. She arrived in Oklahoma one year after "The Great Run."

The Great Run took place before Oklahoma became a state. People were lined up on the Kansas-Oklahoma border. At a signal, they ran out into Oklahoma to get free land. Whatever land you settled on was yours to homestead, free. Those who got all that free land found oil on it, too! Naturally, our family showed up the next year, when it was all over.

Dave Galoob was a peddler who came into our mama's store.

They got to know each other over time, and they were married in the early 1900s. Mama's name was Rebecca Ammerman Kins Galoob. Celia and Jack's father was Sam Kins. Milton, Sarah, and Rivka's father was Dave Galoob, but we were raised as one family. Our mother had ten children in all, but she only raised five. Oklahoma was a wild place back then. There were no doctors. There were no medications. People didn't go to the hospital to have a baby. They stayed in the house. If there were complications, there was nothing to be done.

Reva was born on Armistice Day. Celia got up early that morning to get the younger kids off to school. We all knew something strange was happening, because Celia never got up that early in her life. The school took us to see the Armistice Day Veteran's Parade. It was an exciting parade with flags flying, bands playing, and veterans marching, but our father came to get us before the parade ended. He came to take us home to meet our new baby. We were so excited about the parade we didn't want to leave. We said, "Baby? What baby? Who cares?" Finally, after much coaxing, we agreed to go home. We found baby Reva lying up in the bed with our mother. She was a gorgeous baby!

There was no Temple in Wewoka, Oklahoma, when we were growing up, but our family always found a way to maintain our Jewish identity. The older children went to Synagogue in Tulsa, Oklahoma, with our father. Mama didn't go because she had to stay home with the little ones, Milton and Reva. Jewish people wanted to give their children a religious education, so we met in different places for our religious classes. Our first Sunday school class was taught at the courthouse. Our teacher was Sarah Sobol. If you want to know how close the Jewish people of the oilfield were, Sarah Sobol later became Sarah Rabicoff of Kilgore!

Our parents were "Boomers." They followed the boom, opening stores in all the little oilfield boomtowns. When we came to Longview we were accustomed to living in boomtowns because we grew up in all the booms of Oklahoma.

The young Jewish people of this oil boom town continued to stay together after they were married. A ladies' mah-jong group played at Annette Felsenthal's house. They were all pregnant at the same time. They were all so large that none of them could reach the table. Annette Felsenthal had to pick up the tiles for them. Annette had her baby first, though, because she adopted Danny!

Minnie and Milton Galoob pose with their daughter, Debbie, at her marriage to Peter Rugh.
—Photo courtesy Sandi Sachnowitz

Marguerite Balter had her daughter Harriet on July 10. Then Minnie Galoob had her daughter, Debbie. Sarah's son, Mike, was born next, and Bea Andres had her son, David, after that, one right after the other. They were three weeks apart. Bessie Feldman had her son, Larry, shortly afterward. Six Jewish kids were born in Longview in short order, and all six of them graduated in the top of their high school class.

A group of older ladies played bingo, although they called it "Bingle." Mama Galoob used to tell her grandchildren she would buy them a "station waggle" so they could drive her to the "bingle" games.

The "Bingle" ladies included Mama Galoob, Mrs. Riff, Mrs. Booken, Mrs. Daiches, and Mrs. Leibson. They were very formal, and they never used their first names. They always called each other "Mrs." Later, after their health was bad and most of them had to walk with walkers, they still continued to play "bingle"—and they would cheat!

Mrs. Booken could drive, and she drove all over town on Fridays, collecting money for Jewish charities. Mama Galoob would go along as company. Ada Milstein always cleaned her house on Fridays, and Mama Galoob used to say that Ada was the only proper housekeeper in East Texas. When she went to visit, Mama Galoob would reach down between the sofa cushions to see what was stuck in the furniture. If there was any grit, she would say this woman wasn't a good housekeeper. But she never found any grit at Ada Milstein's house, so Ada was her favorite.

Mama Galoob was a fanatic about cleanliness. When the family got out of a bed in the morning she would turn the mattress. Not only did the sheet get changed, the mattress got turned every day. The bedclothes came off and were hung out in the yard to air.

She had three washing machines, one for underwear, one for bed sheets, and one for other stuff. Mama Galoob was clean, she was a good businesswoman, she had many talents, but she wasn't a cook. When Norman Balter first started selling insurance to our family, he would sit at the table and drink her coffee. The family figured he really wanted to sell that insurance, because her coffee was awful! She never had time to learn to be a good cook because she was always in business. She never had the opportunity for a formal education. She couldn't read or write until her grandchildren taught her how to sign her name, but she could do arithmetic. Give her a list of figures and she would come up with the right answer. She spoke broken English, but her Yiddish was excellent. She sat on a velvet chair in Celia's store every day, and she knew everything that was going on in town. She didn't miss a thing.

She was a remarkable woman. She had tremendous courage. If anything went wrong when her children were young, she would keep it from them and bear the burden herself. If one of her children had anything at all, he or she was expected to contribute part of it to help the others. She'd finagle the one who could give, and share it with the one who didn't have anything. That way, everybody had a little something to get by. It was the depression. There was plenty of finagling going on in order to survive.

That was then, and this is now, and there is still a lot of finagling going on in East Texas. The boom may be gone, but East Texas hasn't changed that much!

CHAPTER 12

DeDe Gans

The oil boom started in 1930, so it was well under way by the time I arrived in Longview. The big oil companies had bought up all the leases they could get their hands on, but this was still a wild and wooly place. It was busy and bustling, and of course everything else in the country was in bad shape. East Texas was one of the few bright spots in the United States.

The "lease hounds" used to meet at the hotel. You could recognize them by the way they dressed and talked. The lease hounds took advantage of a lot of people. They certainly cheated the black people who owned land. They'd offer them a thousand dollars for the lease on their acreage. A thousand dollars looked like a million in the 1930s, and many of the landowners agreed. That thousand dollars has long been spent, but oil is still coming out of the ground in many of those acres.

At Christmastime, Kilgore had big Christmas stars on all the derricks downtown. That was a sight you'd never see in this world! They tore down half a church and half a bank to put up wells. Everyone who came to East Texas wanted to see the oil wells in downtown Kilgore.

I was born and raised in Little Rock, Arkansas. My mother was born in Baltimore, and my father came from Hungary as a young boy. He said they used to move the boundary lines back and forth so often that nobody ever really knew exactly where they were living, but it was Hungary the year he was born.

My parents, Sophie and William Back Sr., had seven children. Our name was originally Bach, but it made life easier for everyone when they changed it so it would be spelled the way it sounded.

There were quite a number of Jewish families living in Little Rock. The story is that Memphis, Tennessee, had been the stopping line for immigration, but there was some kind of fever raging in Memphis so a lot of the Jewish people came across the Mississippi River and remained in Arkansas. Most were merchants who opened little businesses. My grandfather owned a store. When he passed away, my father and my two uncles took it over. Years ago you could come into a town, open a store, and settle there, but that's a thing of the past, because the big stores and chain stores have eaten the small stores up.

My husband, Leon, was also born in Little Rock, and I had known him all my life. He came to Longview in 1934 with his partner, Nap Scher, Nap's wife Sally, and their daughter Ilaine, and they opened Gans' Men's Store downtown. Nap Scher was Carrie Riff's brother, so Carrie told him about the opportunities here. Leon later bought his partner out.

Leon's father had died, but his sister and his mother, May Gans, were still living in Little Rock. When he came home to see them, he would take me out. We were married in Little Rock, and I arrived in Longview as a bride. Sam Dorfman's wife, Elizabeth, introduced me to people and made me feel at home. You might say that she "sponsored" me, which was very fortunate for me. Although we had a number of Jewish people in the oil business, many Jewish people came to East Texas to open small retail businesses. That way, many of us made a living as a result of the oil, but not directly from it.

If you close your eyes and imagine the buildings in downtown Longview, you can almost read the names of the Jewish merchants who had stores there. It was a close community. The men would meet at the Longview Drugstore for coffee every morning before they opened the shops.

The roughnecks and oilfield workers might not have had much schooling, but they were hard-working people and they were making a lot of money for the first time in their lives. Money was free-flowing from the bottom to the top. We sold moderate-priced merchandise at Leon's store, but other stores in town sold finer lines.

When they first struck oil, some of the people went a little bit overboard in the things they would buy and the things they would do, but you couldn't blame them. They didn't have anything for such a long time, and suddenly money was pouring in. They were getting rich in oil at two dollars a barrel! That's a lot of oil and a lot of money. I remember how the daughters of one oilman would see an ad in the Dallas paper for something expensive and wonderful, like a diamond pin. They wouldn't check on it or anything, they would just call the shop on the phone and have it sent out!

People here always dressed well. We took the Dallas paper, which was full of Neiman Marcus ads. Neiman Marcus was a frontrunner of fashion and had a great influence on East Texas. Neiman's was nationally known, and having Neiman's so close set the pace for us. Riff's and Martin's here were lovely stores with high-quality merchandise, but since Dallas was so close, a group of us would take the train to Dallas to shop and have lunch and really make a day of it. Then we would come home on the evening train.

Carrie Riff and Celia Bergman worked in their stores, but most of the women didn't work. We had a lovely social life. We went to coffees or luncheons and teas, and we played mah-jong and cards.

I had a maid and paid her a dollar a day, and I spent a dollar a day for food. She was a talented cook who fixed the best meals, wonderful fried chicken and the best biscuits! She had a table full of vegetables, and we hardly ever had dinner that company didn't come by to eat with us. All on a dollar a day! Although that sounds as though she was terribly underpaid, we were really not taking advantage of her. A dollar was a lot of money in those depression days. We weren't earning much more than she was. We were working, and she was working. People were proud to do any sort of honest work back then. Television wasn't invented yet, so on Saturday nights everyone would come to town and stroll up and down the streets to shop and visit, or stop in at the drugstore for coffee or ice cream. You'd see everybody you knew. It was like a big party every weekend.

The stores would stay open late on Saturday nights, but when they closed, our group would all meet at Mattie's Ballroom or go out for dinner. We were delighted when Johnny Cace's Seafood Restaurant opened its first little location downtown, because that was our first really good place to eat. The old Longview Hotel was one of Hilton's first hotels, and they had a good dining room. We often had dinners at each other's homes. We had a "Sunday Night Club" where

Members of Temple Emanu-El of Longview enjoy a special holiday celebration. Right to left: Millie Brin, Dave Bergman, DeDe Gans, Phyllis Feldman, Ann Balter, Irene Dworin, David Hirsch, and Joy Wolf.

—Photo courtesy Gordon Balter

we would take turns serving dinner. After dinner, the women would play mah-jong or bridge and the men would play poker. Every once in a while one of the Jewish couples would have a party at Romeo's Restaurant on the Kilgore Highway.

We belonged to the Pinecrest Country Club, which was unusual in a time when anti-Semitism was an accepted fact of life in most places, and religious segregation was practiced in most country clubs. It wasn't like that here. We were part of the community. We were known because of our stores downtown and also because of our civic work. Many of us were active in the community and respected.

People like Dave Bergman did so much for the Boy Scouts and the hospital and every good activity in town, and of course we all contributed to community works. We gave whatever we could. When we couldn't afford to give money, we gave our time.

Although there were a lot of Jewish people in Little Rock, there were only four other Jewish kids at Central High School when I graduated in a class of six hundred. Leon and I were comfortable with

Christians. Someone coming here from a place like New York might not be as comfortable because they'd probably never seen a Christian up close before. In a place like Little Rock or Longview, you tend to look past the differences and see the person. Leon and I had Christian friends when we were growing up, and we had Christian friends here.

We played cards or bridge with Bess McCann. Johnny Gasway and her daughter, Jerry Lindsay, were great friends of mine. Johnny was a pillar of the First Baptist Church, and she had a lot of Jewish friends. Although Johnny used to say her husband never went into a store to shop for anything in his life, Bob Gasway would come into our store to visit with us every chance he'd get. They were such fine people, such good friends, I think about them all the time and I miss them terribly.

When World War II started, most of the younger Jewish men were called into the service. Abe Silverman and Bernie Weinstein were among them. The older men, like Dave Bergman and Joe Riff, were not called to the army, but their employees were. Even though my husband Leon was not called up, the men who worked for us were, and so he needed my help. I had to go to work. The war brought a change in everybody's lives. Women took over and carried on the businesses.

The Lone Star Steel Company made munitions in Daingerfield, a few miles north of Longview. Quite a few Jewish people came with them, but they didn't stay long.

Harmon Military Hospital was located where LeTourneau College is now. We had groups that would go to the Harmon Hospital and take things to the Jewish boys who were bedridden. The Rabbi would come from Marshall to see about them.

We didn't have a Temple in Longview, but we had services for the Jewish people who were at the hospital, the army officers, their families, and the patients. We had a lot of soldiers here, and we did everything we could to make them welcome. The Jewish people who came with the army were very nice. We knew they couldn't stay long, once they were gone, they were gone, but they were welcome while they were here.

When a new group would come in to the hospital, they would see the Jewish names on the stores downtown so they would come into the store and introduce themselves. They were from all over the country. A lot of them were from the Northeast. You know how the army likes to mix them up? They sent the southern boys north and the northern boys south. They were so hungry for any kind of Jewish contact, anything they could recognize and make them feel at home. Our community "adopted" them. We would have them over for dinner and to visit with the family. Whenever we would go into Dallas, we would bring back a little something, a piece of salami or corned beef, and they would go wild over it. They couldn't buy anything like that here.

One Passover, we held a Seder for them at the Longview Community Center downtown. We cooked all the food at home, carted it down there, and served it hot. We served about a hundred people for dinner.

We all did our part. We had ten or twelve troop trains a day stop here with hundreds of soldiers on them. Longview's women would organize, and we had different days when would go to the station. We would take doughnuts and coffee and cake.

When the boys got off the train to stretch their legs, they would just stare. Many of them thought they'd see cowboys and horses on the streets of Texas. Others thought they had come to the end of the world. It was so sad. These young kids were so far away from home, many for the first time in their lives. They were pulled up by their roots from all ends of the country. We'd talk to them and make them feel a little better, if only for a while. There were quite a few Jewish boys, and they were surprised to find us here!

It was wartime and we all had to do our share. The whole city worked together. The Jewish people participated with the rest of the community. The Jewish ladies worked right along with the Gray Ladies and the Red Cross. We had so much to do, with the Harmon Hospital and the troop trains coming through, we didn't ever stop. The few little extra things we did for the Jewish boys, well, that was something we felt we had to do.

We had our Red Cross Headquarters in the old Everett Bank Building where the Gregg County Historical Museum is now located. We all knitted stocking caps for the soldiers to protect them when they were cold. They had a little slit in them so that they could see out. Just their eyes and a little bit of their faces would show. We made hundreds and hundreds of sweaters. The Red Cross gave us khaki-colored yarn and patterns, and the ladies would go up there and knit. When I wasn't working at the store, I went and did what I could.

My brother Eddie was in the service in Midland. He'd come in on the train on Friday night. We'd pick him up at the train station and we'd go out to the honkeytonks. Then we'd put him back on the train Sunday morning. We liked to go to a place called "Satchel City" near Lake Devernia. It was on the slope just before you go into Gladewater on the Gladewater Highway. It was pure East Texas screen-door honkeytonk, where you could smell the beer out in the street. One night, they wouldn't let my brother in. A soldier was killed there the week before and it was "off-limits" to military personnel. So we went up the road to a place called "Curley's." Someone was shot while we were there. They called the police to come pick him up. Then they just moved the body out of the way and kept right on dancing!

Life was fairly settled in town, but it was wild in the honkeytonks. Milton Galoob was in the beer business, and he delivered beer to all the honkeytonks. When I came here as a bride I had some very nice clothes from my trousseau, but we'd go out to Mattie's Ballroom, and since they never had a sidewalk out in the country, I'd get mud all over my shoes and the bottoms of my skirts. Still, Mattie's was the best place to go. Mattie would bring the big bands from all over the country. She always kept things from getting rowdy and wild.

Before we had our Temple in Longview, we went to Temple Moses Montifiore in Marshall for the High Holy Days. Leon had been here for several years before we married, and since he had always gone to Marshall, that's where I went. It was sometimes an adventure because the roads were not great.

Although it wasn't very large, Temple Moses Montifiore was beautiful, with a magnificent pipe organ and lovely stained-glass windows. The woodwork had wonderful dark carvings. They always had a dignified service. I have happy memories of worshipping there. The Ark and Bimah rail as well as the everlasting light are now in the possession of the Marshall Historical Museum.

The Temple in Marshall only had a tiny little kitchen, because except for Passover Seder they never served anything. They did have wonderful Seder suppers. It's interesting that they never had an Oneg Shabbat reception after services like we do here in Longview.

When services ended, the people would visit in front of the Temple for a little while and then everyone would just go home.

My congregation in Little Rock never had an Oneg Shabbat reception, either. Perhaps that's the different custom in different places, but you miss a lot of pleasant fellowship that way. Here in Longview, we always have coffee and cake and have a little party after services on Friday night. It's nice to get together and visit with the other people.

The group of us who went to Marshall were friendly with the people there, but I think the people who went to Kilgore were friendlier. Congregation Beth Shalom in Kilgore had a more Orthodox group. Hymie Hurwitz and Max Daiches or some of the other men led the services. They had different rabbis from time to time. At first they held their services in a store, then in the city hall, and finally, in 1936, they were able to build their building.

They had a nice Jewish community in Marshall, but many of the older people died and others moved away so that the congregation slowly dwindled. The Kilgore congregation grew, so we started to go there. Dan Kerman was rabbi then, and he was a wonderful person. The time came when the congregation outgrew their building. Since many more of us lived in Longview, we wanted to build our new building here. We have had to work hard for every brick in that building. You might say Temple Emanu-El of Longview is the daughter of the Kilgore Temple.

There were times when we didn't have a rabbi at all and being Jewish was a "do it yourself" project, but you always got as much out of it as you put into it. When you live in a smaller community, you make the Jewish experience what you want it to be. In a large city, where you may be one of thousand members of a congregation, many people can't take advantage of opportunities for Jewish life. Here, each one of us is important. We all take part in everything. You can be rich or poor, educated or uneducated, but if you are a decent person, you are welcomed with open arms like a long-lost relative. I've liked my life here. I have good friends, and that's a good feeling.

CHAPTER 13

Phillip Hurwitz

"It was a time like no other time and a place like no other place that ever was, or ever will be again."

My strongest impression of the early days in Kilgore was the image of thick red clay. There were no sidewalks, just boards. If you wanted to cross the street, you'd have to walk on boards. When the boards were wet from the rain and you slipped, you would be up to your knees in the mud. You'd have to struggle to get yourself out. It was horrible! Just muck and mire! The boom started in 1930, and it rained all the time that year.

It's hard to imagine how crude everything was, just like the Wild West movies. Most of the oilmen used mules and wagons to carry pipe and equipment to the oil wells. If it was raining they wouldn't dare use their mules, because even the mules would bog down in that red clay mud. You could say it was miserable living, but at the same time, it was fantastic. It was like nothing else in the world. There was so much going on! It was a great experience for a young boy.

There were nine children in my family, five boys and four girls, Lena, Sam, Ethel, Ann, Hyman, Frieda, William, Sidney, and Phillip. We all looked like our mother. Mother had had a very fair complexion, with pink, rosy cheeks. She was prematurely gray. We all were.

In fact, the Hurwitz appearance was so easily identifiable that we could be recognized completely across the world.

During World War II, when I was in the service in India, I heard two sergeants talking and there was no way to mistake their Texas accent. I heard one of them say "Fort Worth," and of course my ears perked up at the mention of my hometown. I asked if they were from Fort Worth. The sergeant took one look at me and said, "I don't know who you are, but I know you're a Hurwitz!" Our family resemblance was that strong.

Pop's name was Morris, and mom's name was Ida. Pop was in the poultry business in Fort Worth. He originally came from Russia, and my mom came from just across the river in Austria. When they were young, Pop used to swim across that river in order to court Mom and then swim back home again. Isn't that a grand romantic story?

My oldest brother, Sam, opened a men's clothing store in Kilgore when the boom first started. After a year, he put my brother Hyman to work running the Kilgore store while he opened a store in Gladewater. When I was sixteen, I started coming to East Texas to help the "boys" during my summer vacations.

The town was booming and business was good. They couldn't just find people who knew anything about selling men's clothing, so they needed me. Mom would fix me a corned beef sandwich in a paper sack and I'd get on the train in Fort Worth. My brothers would pick me up at the Gladewater station and I'd go to work. Then, when my three months of summer "vacation" were over, I'd get back on the train and go home and back to school in Fort Worth. At Christmastime, I'd return to East Texas to help my brothers with their Christmas business. That was my Christmas "vacation" in the oilfield.

The first Kilgore store was quite long, but it was only twenty-five feet wide. That was pretty typical for stores of that time and in that place. It had a high ceiling, with wooden floors and dark wooden fixtures. Two heavy-set men couldn't pass each other comfortably in that store.

There were tables with pants and khakis stacked up high, according to size. We had hats stacked on top of the fixtures all the way to the ceiling. You'd have to take them down with what they called a "hat stick." This was a long stick with a kind of round gadget at one end. You'd put the round part up under the boxes and take them down very carefully. There was something of an art to it. Before I learned how to do it properly, I spilled hats all over the floor. I certainly would hear about it when that happened.

The amazing thing is that these days, if a house or a store is not air-conditioned, even if you're walking around in short sleeves you're absolutely miserable. We had to wear a coat and tie when we went to work in the store, and we didn't have any air-conditioning. All we had were those big ceiling fans that turned the hot air around and around. We felt fortunate to have these big fans to "cool" us. All they did was blow hot air, but since we didn't know any better, we thought we were comfortable.

Today, you sell the gas from a gas well. Everybody wants to get in on a good gas well. But during the boom they didn't know what to do with the gas, so they'd just burn it in huge flares next to the wells. Those flares burned all night and all day. Nightime was just like daytime in Kilgore. There were so many wells being drilled and so many flares going that it was always light and bright. The fires were hot, but it was already hot in the summer, so what difference could those fires make?

You'd hear these drilling rigs banging and clanging and drilling all day and all night, but you can get used to anything. It was too hot to close the windows against the noise. It didn't matter. If you were tired enough, you slept. A lot of the time if he was too busy or too tired, or if the weather was too bad to go home, Hyman would just go to sleep on top of the khaki pants in the store.

It was difficult to find a place to live. People were living in tents, in lean-to shacks, even in chicken coops. Sam lived at the little rinkey-dink hotel in Gladewater. He never married, so it was convenient and comfortable for him. In later days he moved over to the Longview Hotel.

At first, Hyman had a little room in Kilgore, but by the time I started coming to help him he had married Eva. They were lucky enough to have a little house, and I lived with them. You had to be lucky to find a house in Kilgore in those days. If somebody had any place to rent, you thought it was a palace. Eva was an elegant girl, but she survived in less-than-elegant surroundings because they were young and they were trying to make a future for themselves. They knew they could do it if they persevered and worked hard enough.

We'd open the store at six-thirty or seven o'clock in the morning because a lot of drillers and roughnecks went to work at that hour and they might need to buy a suit of khakis, or some rubber boots. For the most part, that's all we sold in the first store: khakis, Stetson hats, rubber boots, cowboy boots, and a few suits. We'd sell slicker suits and waterproof coats and hats and pants to protect the men so they could work out on the drilling rigs in all kinds of weather.

We'd close the store at nine, ten, eleven o'clock at night, whenever the last man was off the street. Then we would go out to Mattie's Ballroom and we'd dance the night away. In the earliest days, Mattie had taxi dancers. You'd buy a roll of tickets for five dollars, pick out a pretty girl, give her your tickets, and dance with her all evening. They were wonderful dancers. After working all day and dancing all night, we'd go home around five in the morning, take a bath, lie down for an hour to rest, get up, and go back to work. We thought we were having lots of fun.

Mattie Castleberry was the Mattie of Mattie's Ballroom. She was quite a girl. She ran a clean place. You didn't feel uncomfortable going there. Nobody messed with her. She wouldn't tolerate abusive or vulgar language. If there was a fight brewing, she would ask the participants to leave. She would tell them to do all the fighting they wanted, but to do it outside.

The rest of the oilfield wasn't quite so orderly. At one point things were so bad with looting and running hot oil that they had to declare martial law. The Texas Rangers set a curfew. Everyone had to be off the streets by six o'clock.

My brother Hyman was working late. He was a man of the community and he wasn't even thinking about doing anything wrong, so he thought the Rangers wouldn't bother him. But no sooner did he close the store and step out of the door than Texas Ranger "Lone Wolf" Gonzaullas picked him up.

"Lone Wolf" used to look at a man's hands. If they were soft and cared for, not rough like an oilman's hands, "Lone Wolf" suspected the man was a crook, a gambler, a gunman . . . or worse. That was a time when they didn't have a jail in Kilgore. The Texas Rangers had set out a big pole with metal chains in front of the Baptist church. "Lone Wolf" handcuffed Hyman to that chain, and he stayed there until he was convinced that he had to be off the streets just like everybody else. It must have been a shock to him. When they heard where he was, several of the Jewish people in town came out and vouched for him.

My brother Hyman had a tremendous personality. Everybody in Kilgore loved him. Both my brothers created a wonderful following. They were honest. They never misled their customers. People respected their integrity. Hyman and Sam taught me to extend all the courtesies that you possibly can to customers and salesmen alike.

Over in Tyler, they already had an established Jewish community. Tyler's Reform Temple Beth-El celebrated its centennial in 1987, and I don't know how much older it is than Tyler's more Orthodox Ahavath Achim Synagogue. But there wasn't any organized Jewish activity in Kilgore during the earliest days. Still, Jewish people were coming to Kilgore, establishing businesses and pipe yards and becoming involved in drilling for oil. The Jews who came during the boom did not turn their backs on their Judaism. They did everything they could to keep their religious life together. The men would hold Minyans in their stores. As soon as they could, they established religious schools and held classes in their stores. As the oilfield became more "civilized," they had Passover Seders in their homes, and as soon as it was possible, they organized Temple Shalom.

A woman named Anne Rose was instrumental in getting things started. Her husband, Bernard, was in the scrap metal business, and she called a meeting of the Jewish women at their house behind their yard. Her idea was to form a Women's Auxiliary so they could start a formal Sunday school for the children. The idea for a Temple came from that meeting.

They built a little building in 1936 and were able to hire a rabbi. They celebrated every Sabbath and all the holidays and had nice community functions. Some of the charter members included Sam Goldman, Harry Golden, Sol Finkelstein, Joe Waldman, Max Daiches, Sam Dorfman. Smiley Rabicoff, and my brothers, Hyman and Sam Hurwitz.

My brother Hyman was responsible for the synagogue having a rather unusual Social Hall. There was a little frame gambling house out at Lake Devernia where men would go at night to drink, shoot dice, play poker, and such. Hyman happened to be there when they were talking about tearing that little building down and putting up a new one. He asked what they wanted for the building. They set a

Workers on an oil rig.

—Fowler Studio photo

price. The congregation bought the building, had it moved next to the Temple, refurbished it, and made it their Social Hall.

Tyler had Jewish dances at the Mayfair Building on the Fair Grounds. It was a big, barnlike building, and Jewish young people came from all over East Texas and western Louisiana to dance on Saturday night. They used to come to these dances from Dallas and Fort Worth.

Before World War II, I was taking a pre-law course at Texas Christian University. I finished TCU, then went on to the University of Texas at Austin. I was in law school for two years when the war broke out. As luck would have it, I had a very low draft number. That summer, I went to the draft board in Fort Worth to see if they would allow me to be deferred for a year so that I could complete my law work. They refused.

I didn't want to go into the infantry, so I signed up for the Air Corps. I didn't go back to school that September because I had been told that in another month or so they would send me to the Air Corps. Instead, I went back to Kilgore and went to work for my brother.

I was called up, but I was turned down. Apparently, they had some young doctor who couldn't read x-rays and said I had tubercular spots on my lungs. I'd never had tuberculosis. Either he read somebody else's x-rays, or there were water spots on the films. I don't know what he thought he saw, but there I was, turned down for the army, but I'd already signed up for the Air Corps! I figured if the army turned me down the Air Corps would do likewise, because they were far more strict. For the most part, the army was taking anybody who could walk through the door.

That December, I was called to Fort Worth, where the Air Corps had set up testing equipment at the Texas Hotel. There were sixty-seven of us taking the physical exam. I was one of the seventeen out of the sixty-seven who passed the physical. They put me on a troop train and shipped me to Kelley Field that night. I had to call Hyman from San Antonio to ask him to close up my apartment and do the best he could with my clothes and stuff.

I served a little more than five years in the Air Corps. I was in India a little more than two years. I was head of lend lease and reciprocal aid, purchasing and contracts for all the air forces in the China-Burma-India theater. I had a very important job at a very young age.

Young as I was, I was on the General Staff. I was well respected. I got my orders from Washington. I did a lot of work with the Indian government and the British government. I had a DC-3 aircraft assigned to me because the British Government and the Indian Government were headquartered in New Delhi. I had to fly there frequently to make demands on those two governments for items the Air Corps needed that were indigenous to either country.

In turn, I would accommodate them by getting them American parts or whatever they needed. I made lots of friends in the Indian Government and received a number of honors. When you're young, and these honors are bestowed upon you, they're impressive. I was given the Bronze Star. I received lots of commendations. I was promoted, and I retired as a Lieutenant Colonel. They said I was able to accomplish something, to contribute to the war effort. Perhaps it's because I put forth the same amount of effort as I did in the store in Kilgore. When I undertake a job I always try to do it to the best of my ability.

When the war was over, having been to India and other places and having had a position of importance, I didn't want to go back to school. I came home to Kilgore. My brothers needed me here. Business was good. Everybody was doing well, and I wanted to live well. I wanted a good future. More than anything else, I wanted a car, so I saved my money and bought my first convertible.

Kilgore had grown. It wasn't as primitive as it had been when the boom first came in. They had a City Commission. They had paved streets and lights on the corners. Over a period of time, the place became a little more modern, a little more up to the times. I was doing well in Kilgore. My brother Sid returned from the war and went to work in the Gladewater store. We opened a store in Longview and later in Texarkana. We tried to get Hyman and Sam to go in with us, but they didn't want to expand anymore, so eventually Sid and I went in to business for ourselves in Tyler.

None of my experiences in Kilgore made me feel different because I was Jewish. The Jewish people were always an accepted and important part of in the community. Of course, Hyman participated in every civic function the city had. He was on a number of local boards and civic boards. He was past president of the Chamber of Commerce. Later in life, they used to call him "Mr. Kilgore."

All of the Jews in Kilgore and Longview participated in activities and became part of the community. We identified with our neighbors, but at the same time we had our own religion, and we practiced it the best way we could. We respected our neighbors for who they were, and our neighbors respected us for who we were.

My only problem was meeting Jewish girls. There simply weren't any Jewish girls in Kilgore. Nathan Waldman and I were dear, close friends, and we went many places together to meet Jewish girls before I met Jean and he met his wife Florence and brought her home to Kilgore. We would travel to Shreveport two or three times a week. It was inconvenient. The roads weren't wonderful. When you're young, driving sixty miles across the state on questionable roads doesn't bother you because you don't have that much sense. We'd go out and have a good time in Shreveport, then hit the road about one or two o'clock in the morning and get back about three or three-thirty. By then, things were more civilized and we weren't opening the stores until eight-thirty or nine o'clock.

I met my wife Jean when I sang at a wedding in Kilgore. Jean's father, Mr. Sugar, had put the bride and groom into the pipe business here. I knew Mr. Sugar through drilling some wells. I had asked for his advice from time to time. Afterward, somebody came into the store and said, "You ought to court that girl."

I said, "She's a little young. She lives in Shreveport. She's going to school," and so on until I made enough excuses. Then I thought about it and I said, "Oh, she is really pretty." But I didn't do anything.

Six months after that, I was flying to Birmingham to sing at another wedding. There were two lovely girls sitting in front of me, paying no attention to me whatsoever. When we landed at Shreveport, I saw Mr. Sugar. I asked what he was doing there, and he said he had come to pick up his daughter. Lo and behold, there was Jean, getting off the plane. We chatted for a few moments and I thought, Well, she is pretty, maybe I ought to call her?

When I got back from Birmingham, I called and asked if she would like to go out with me. I had created quite a fast reputation for myself in Shreveport. Among other things, I was driving a light blue Buick convertible, which I always drove with the top down. It was first Buick convertible in East Texas.

Jean thought, He drives a big convertible, he wears a big star sapphire on his finger, he's older and he's been around a lot. And she knew that she was young. She said, "I don't know if I can go out with you." But I was persistent. Finally she said, "I'll meet you for a drink on Saturday." I thought she meant we would go to a bar and have a drink. Then she said, "But the only way I'll go with you is if you bring your brother and sister-in-law along."

I might have had a reputation for being pretty fast, but I really wasn't. I was an honorable young fellow. I asked, "What night can we come over?"

She said, "No, I want you to come over in the afternoon."

I thought it strange that this nice young girl wanted to go drinking in the afternoon. Then she told me she wanted to go to the drugstore and drink a soda!

I said, "You've got to be kidding."

She said, "No, because that's the only way I'll go out with you, and you'll have to bring your brother Bill and his wife Sally with you, too."

By this time I really wanted to go out with her, so we all had an ice-cream soda in a drugstore and then she went home. I called her again and again. Finally, I broke the ice and we started going out. I took her out a great deal.

About that time I took a sabbatical from the men's clothing business to get involved in the oil business. Hyman, Sam, Bill, and I were all involved, but they let me handle it. It was hard because everything in the oil business was done way out in the boondocks where the mosquitoes were as big as your thumb. There were no roads. Even my little jeep would bog down in the mud and I'd have to get a bulldozer to pull me out. You had to walk to where the wells were, and it was a miserable existence. You might have to go couple of miles off the road to the place where you thought there might be oil. You'd have to hack down trees and lay boards down to improvise a road. When it rained, your improvised road turned to solid mud.

Today, you can drive along the highway and see wells all pumping away at the side of the road. When wells were drilled here in Kilgore, they were out in the woods. Those highways were not there. Over a period of time when they built a highway, it just so happened that the road would be next to somebody's well. When it was originally being drilled, it was hell to get out to those places.

You trusted geologists and engineers to find your wells. They would take core samples and analyze them and decide whether it looked like it would be productive sand. To get a core sample, they would drill and take a core of the formation and study the formation.

They knew that there is a possibility of oil being in certain sands and certain strata. Of course I don't know how they would find the particular spot and say, "Let's drill here, or let's drill there." That was their job. They studied petroleum engineering and geology and they knew how to do it.

I was living at the Shreve Hotel and doing some oil work in Oil City, right outside Shreveport, where we had a lease. I forget how many acres it was, but we had to drill it. There were shallow wells. I bought all the equipment and made the contracts with the drillers to equip it after the well came in.

Then, after I was going out with Jean for two or three years, I picked up and went out to California. Marty Lancer, a friend I'd met in the service, was living in Hollywood. He kept calling me to come out there and go in with him on some productions. I decided it sounded interesting, so I did it. We had a documentary film company. In fact, I have the brochure for our first production, which was for the UAW-AFofL. It was called *In the Good Old Days*, and the narrator was none other than our former president, Ronald Reagan, who was then president of the Screen Actor's Guild.

I stayed out there for eleven months, but you know the old adage, "You can take the boy out of the country but you can't take the country out of the boy." I didn't like the life that I was leading in Hollywood. It was faster than the oilfield ever thought about being. There was wine, women, and song. Some people loved it, but I couldn't see myself continuing to like that, because I knew it would have made an old man of me before my time. My brothers kept telling me they needed me, so I came home.

I was in Dallas, walking across the street from the Adolphus Hotel to the Baker Hotel, when I ran into Jean. We had coffee and she wanted to know why I picked up and left. I told her I didn't know. I had the opportunity to go to Hollywood and it just seemed like the thing to do at the time. I started courting her again, and we were married by Rabbi Dan Kerman at the Beth Sholom Synagogue in Kilgore. We were the first marriage he performed.

If you look around the neat, orderly city of Kilgore, with its beautiful college campus, its cultural activities, symphony performances, and lovely homes, it's hard to imagine what it was like during the oil boom. It was a time like no other time and a place like no other place that ever was, or ever will be again.

CHAPTER 14

Louis Kariel Sr.

"It didn't take long to find out when they hit a dry hole. You knew it right away because the oil didn't come in."

I wasn't smart when the oil boom happened. I didn't get in on it right away. Quite a few of the Jewish people in Marshall were involved in oil royalties and did well. My cousin Harry Feltman persuaded me to get involved in two or three wells that turned out to be happy experiences. Henry Stein, who worked next door to me in town, took part on a number of royalties. One time I got together with my cousin and Harry Stein and a few other people and we got a lease. Unfortunately, our lease helped to define the edge of the field. It didn't take long to find out when they hit a dry hole. You knew it right away because the oil didn't come in.

The same group went in on a well in a little field at a placed called Rodessa. We went there to watch what we hoped would be the completion of the well. We watched as they brought in a bunch of saltwater. We helped define the edge of the field on that one, too.

I grew up in Marshall and was confirmed at Temple Moses Montifiore. We had a beautiful Reform Temple and we usually were fortunate enough to have a Rabbi. Jewish people were active in Marshall politically and in business, but we were not accepted socially at all when I was growing up. That was a long time ago. Thank goodness, things have changed dramatically since that time!

I wasn't big enough to play football or take part in any of the other athletic teams when I was in high school, so I was in the Debating Society and other such activities. I was friendly with all the other children in my class, but my closest friends were my cousins.

We had a lot of family here when I was growing up. My mother was born in Syracuse, New York, into a large German-Jewish family. Seven of the children lived to become adults. Six of them eventually came to Marshall. Her sisters were Fanny and Carol, and her brother was Sol Weisman, who only lived here for a short time before moving to McKinney.

The good Lord gave me a pretty good intellect, and I was often at the head of my class. My cousin Adrian Marcus was in the same class. I was the highest of the boys, but of course I was nowhere near as high as she was. She graduated as salutatorian of our class.

In those old days of the nineteenth century, Texas was very defi-

Temple Moses Montifiore, Marshall Texas.
—Photo courtesy Audrey and Louis Kariel, Jr.

nitely the Wild West. How did all these New York people arrive in this place? It makes an interesting story. One of the members of my family, Isaac Wolf, of Syracuse, New York, had bad asthma. He heard that moving west would help his asthma so he came to Texas in 1850. He came to Marshall and went into the cotton brokerage business. He became successful, so he encouraged his nephews, Daniel and Mayer Dopplemeyer, to join him. Daniel Dopplemeyer served in the Confederate Army during the War Between the States.

Daniel Dopplemeyer brought his nephew, Joe Weisman, and Joe Weisman brought the rest of his brothers and sisters. Joe opened the Joe Weisman Department Store, and two of the men who worked for him married two of his sisters. His sister Fannie married Mr. Marcus, and my mother married my dad, Morris Kariel.

My dad left Germany and came to America at the age of sixteen. I think he made one trip back to Europe to visit his mother, but other than that he was thrilled to be in America and was proud to be an American. I consider that my father did quite well indeed to have come to this country as a sixteen-year-old immigrant boy who had to learn to do everything in a second language.

My father and Mr. Marcus worked for Joe Weisman at Weisman's Department Store for a long time, until they finally had the opportunity to buy a little clothing store of their own. My father died only a few years after that business was started. He was only fifty-four years old. Shortly after he died, I was drafted into the army to serve in World War I. That was in September 1918. The war was over November 11, 1918. I was in the army, but the war ended before I was needed in combat.

I was educated at the University of Texas, where I majored in chemistry. As soon as I was discharged from the army, I started looking for work as a chemist. I was hired by the Great Western Sugar Company in Sterling, Colorado, and later worked in Cuba as a sugar chemist. From there I got a job in Sugarland, Texas.

I met my wife Adele in Shreveport. My uncle Jake had moved to Shreveport, and we used to visit his family there. My Shreveport cousin used to brag about a special friend named Adele Stein. There was a great deal said about Adele's looks, and with good reason. Adele was beautiful, and she was a sweet woman. We were married by Rabbi Abraham Brill in Shreveport.

With my father gone, my mother was alone in Marshall, and I was concerned for her. Adele and I were in Sugarland, but we both felt that we wanted to come home to be closer to our families. My uncle Mose Weisman owned the Hub Shoe Store in Marshall. He was in his seventies and he wanted to retire. I wanted to come home, where I could take care of my mother and make a living for all of us. I left the chemistry business and bought the Hub Shoe Store from him. I bought it with a partner who had actually worked in the shoe business and knew something about it, which I did not. Adele and I returned home to Marshall and raised our three children, Louis, Stanley, and Maurine, here. We were fortunate and we were successful.

Over the years there were many Jewish "beggars" or "fundraisers" who came through Marshall. They would come to the Jewish merchants, and we would always give them some money. We never knew whether they were legitimate or whether they were frauds, but it didn't really matter. We all felt that it was better to contribute to ten possible frauds than take the chance of letting one needy person suffer.

Much to my surprise, the businessmen of the town asked me to serve on the City Commission in 1933. I considered that to be quite an honor. At that time, the commissioners elected the chairman of the commission as mayor. Some time after the end of my first year, a fine gentleman in town, who was serving as mayor, died. The commissioners asked me to fill his place for one year. That's how I happened to become mayor of Marshall. I was asked to serve, and I was glad to do it. I never ran for mayor. I never ran for anything. I never asked anybody to vote for me. After I served that one year, they elected me chairman of the City Commission, and I continued to serve as mayor for fourteen years until 1947.

Marshall was in the "oil belt" of East Texas. Although many people in Marshall became involved in the oil business, the oil didn't come this way. Therefore, it didn't change Marshall as dramatically as it changed so many of the other cities in our area. We may have fallen a little bit behind other cities for a while, but it isn't going to be that way forever. Marshall is a dynamic city with good people, and we will soon come forward again!

CHAPTER 15

Sam Krasner

I didn't exactly ride into town on a turnip truck the summer of 1930, but my brother Barney and I rode in on a truckload of seven-inch pipe, which we sold to the Fort Worth Pipe and Supply Company in Kilgore. Kilgore had been a small farming town and was not anywhere near big enough to deal with all the activity that happened as soon as oil was discovered. What we saw on that first trip was a booming shack town. Although some of the town's original buildings could still be seen, most of the buildings were hastily constructed of tin or sheet metal.

We made another trip to Kilgore with ten-inch pipe before school started that fall. We were living at Seminole, Oklahoma, and I was a junior at the University of Oklahoma. I later graduated from the University of Oklahoma, class of 1932, with a B.S. in petroleum geology and twenty hours toward my master's degree.

My wife Jene and I were married in 1934, and I was offered a job in a town called Willow Springs, which later became Greggton, and then became part of the Pine Tree area of Longview. While in Willow Springs, I worked for a Jewish manager, Ike Rudman, of the Pittsburgh Pipe and Supply Company.

Besides Ike Rudman, I came to know Sam Roosth and Alex Genecov of Tyler. Smoky Feldman, Sam Goldman, and Dave Isenberg were in the oil business in Gladewater. Smokey Feldman had been in Seminole and knew my father. Harry Golden was my childhood buddy from Tulsa. He worked for another Feldman at Overton.

Ike Hanover had a lease near Overton and promoted a wildcat well near Hallsville. He was jailed for satting, which means putting oil into his well to encourage investors, but I later learned he actually did have a good oil show. I was leaving for Freer in Duval County, Texas, in late 1934. I got together with Jake Jackson, who was the only Jewish trucking contractor in the field. We traded Hanover surface pipe for 100 acres of leases apiece.

There were a couple of Jewish brothers named Newman in Gladewater. Their specialty was completing wells with old-time cable tools.

Besides the Sklars and Phillips, there were a number of other Jewish people from Shreveport involved in the oil business in the East Texas field. I knew the Berry brothers back in Tulsa. Phil, Harry, and Jack were University of Oklahoma graduate geologists. Their older brother Aaron had one lease with three good wells on it back in the early days. Their older sister married Joe Golden, the brother of Harry Golden in Overton.

Joe Gerson managed and was an engineer of H. L. Hunt's Parade Refining Company near Turnertown from 1932 on. Bill Scrinopskie, the Rudmans' son-in-law, came to Gladewater in 1937.

The Travis and Livingston families from Tulsa were cousins and were famous in the early days because they were so observant and kosher. They shut their cable tool drilling rigs down from Friday evening to Saturday evening in observance of the Sabbath. Naturally, this made them very popular with their employees at a time when everybody else in the oilfield worked around the clock seven days a week. The Travises had a long lease that was located along the railroad tracks at Kilgore.

CHAPTER 16

Hyman Laufer

"The National Guard was frequently misled. We would see that the valve on the well indicated that oil was flowing, so we would turn it off. But in fact, the oilmen had cleverly installed valves that worked in reverse."

I was graduated from North Dallas High School in 1930, the year the Great Depression hit. I wanted to go to college, but the failing economy made that seem impossible. Neither of my parents had gone to college, but they had a great respect for education and for learning. Although he lacked a formal education, my father was a very intelligent man who spoke German, Yiddish, Spanish, English, and several other languages. My parents agreed that somehow we would find a way for me to go to school, and I went to North Texas State Teacher's College in Denton. I made my way through school by playing violin in an orchestra. As far as I know, my friend Jack Wood and I were the only Jewish students at North Texas at that time.

Jack told me that if we were to join the National Guard, we could make twenty-one dollars in six weeks during the summer of 1931. Twenty-one dollars was a fortune to us! All we had to do to earn it was to spend six weeks at a camp near Houston. We did that, and all went well. However, while we were riding the train back from camp we began to realize that something was wrong. I asked the conductor why the train was not heading toward Dallas.

He said, "Dallas? No, son, you're not going to Dallas. You're going to East Texas. There's an oilfield out there, and it's turned out to be a terrible place. The governor has ordered the National Guard to put down the troubles."

Our six weeks of summer camp turned out to be a six-month stay in Gladewater. We lived in a tent under a huge oak tree between the office of Jack Phipps and the ice-house.

The governor was obliged to declare martial law and send in the National Guard because law and order had completely broken down. Every thief, every thug, every lawbreaker had found his way into the East Texas oilfield. They were obliged to use the churches for jails, and the churches were always full. More than that, the flood of oil coming out of East Texas was pushing the international price down. The governor declared a maximum allowable amount of oil that could be legally pumped at any given time period. In effect, he shut down the oilfield.

Many of the oilmen didn't like this "allowable" system, and many of them decided to run "hot oil," that is, illegal oil. The National Guard was expected to patrol the oilfield to be sure the wells were not turned on. We were frequently misled. We would go up to a well and see the valve indicated that oil was flowing, so we would turn it off. At least, we thought we had turned it off. In fact, the oilmen had cleverly installed valves that worked in reverse so that we were actually turning it on! There were many other such subterfuges and devices to keep hot oil running.

Every once in a while there was a killing or a shooting. The Texas Rangers patrolled the area as best they could, but they were mostly located in Kilgore. The National Guard patrolled the rest of the oilfield.

They say it rained forty days and forty nights that year, and I am willing to believe it. Mostly, we tried to stay dry. There wasn't much to do when we were not patrolling. Since I don't gamble or shoot craps or play cards, the only thing for me to do was to read. I was stuck in a tent under a tree in the rain and mud in Gladewater, Texas, and so I got a lot of reading done.

My experiences in the National Guard during the oil boom are such a small, insignificant part of my life in East Texas that I hesitate to mention them. Six months is not very much time for a young fellow, and East Texas didn't mean a thing to me except outlaws, hot oil, and mud. Mud was everywhere. Cars got stuck in the mud. Horses and mules got stuck in the mud. I even got stuck in the mud.

If you can visualize an hourglass with the sand trickling down, you would see the shape of the East Texas oilfield, approximately forty-five miles long with Kilgore right at the pinch of the hourglass, and that was where the bulk of the oil was. There were twenty-four derricks on one block of downtown Kilgore, all stuck together with the legs of one derrick right up against the legs of the next. It was called "the World's Richest Acre." This was the largest oilfield in the world until it was superceded by the Arabian oilfields and the North Slope.

I was finally able to return to school and complete my undergraduate work. In 1936, when I completed my graduate work, I went to the University Placement Office looking for a job, but jobs were scarce. The interviewer said, "You're lucky. We just got a call from the superintendent of a little town in East Texas and they need a biology teacher. It pays $90 a month for nine months. Are you interested?"

I said, "Of course I'm interested. Where is it?"

"I'm sure you've never heard of the place," he said. "It's called Gladewater."

So I got on the train, and once again, I was in Gladewater. I walked across the street from the train depot to a little restaurant, which was run by a Jewish man named Scrivnofsky. I said, "I have to spend the night in town, do you have any suggestions?" He suggested the Lee Hotel, and I was able to get a room.

Now, you have to understand that there were rows and rows of oil derricks all up and down the railroad tracks. There were derricks as far and as high as the eye could see. I said, "There's a challenge." The mountain was there and it had to be climbed. Since I knew I was going to do it sooner or later, I thought it was best to get it out of my system as soon as possible and put it behind me. So I put on old khakis and climbed to the top of the first derrick I came to. From the top you could see forever. You could also see how far it was down to earth.

The next morning, I went to work. I taught at Gladewater for three years, from 1936 through 1938. I lived in a little shotgun house with a couple of other young fellows. We did all our own cooking and housekeeping, such as it was. It was not particularly comfortable, but we were lucky to have it, and it was home.

I don't think there were a dozen Jewish families in Gladewater in 1936. Mr. Scrivnofsky owned the little cafe near the railroad depot. Mr. Selman had a drugstore in town. Although he was Jewish, his wife was not and he didn't practice Judaism. There was the oldest Hurwitz brother, Sam. There was the Levinson family.

There were far more families living in Kilgore, and those of us who were interested in prayer came together in Kilgore. In the earliest days, when I was there with the National Guard, we held services in an upstairs room of the old Kilgore City Hall, which was also the fire station. By the time I returned in 1936, they had already built Temple Beth Shalom.

The road between Gladewater and Kilgore was terrible. The road between Gladewater and Longview was awful. Those narrow roads were nothing but oil and mud. People from the towns outside Kilgore were frequently unable to attend Friday-night services because the roads were so bad. Even Highway 80 was a narrow, dangerous road.

I always took the train to Dallas to be with my family for the holidays. Most of the Jewish people had moved from what was then called "North Dallas" to South Dallas. Other ethnic groups, notably African Americans and Hispanics, took our place in the old North Dallas neighborhood.

I left Gladewater to work in Kilgore. In 1940, I met a young lady named Esther whose family lived across the street from my family's home in South Dallas. After supper, almost every night, the women in the community would gather together on Esther's mother's front porch to visit in Yiddish. You could hear them all over South Dallas. My papa fondly called them *yentas* (gossips). Papa used to say, "Oh, there go the *yentas*." Those were good times in South Dallas; it was a good community and a good life.

I didn't pay much attention to Esther while I was in college, because she was just the little neighbor girl who lived across the street. But somehow, while I was away working in Gladewater, she grew up, and I was wise enough to notice that Esther was precious, beautiful, and sweet. I bought a secondhand car and went back and forth on Highway 80 from Kilgore to Dallas every weekend. I courted her for almost a year. We were married at the Tifereth Israel Synagogue in

Dallas, which by that time had relocated near the railroad tracks on Grand Avenue. Ours was the first wedding in the new building.

I brought my lovely bride to Kilgore. Although housing was still scarce, we were fortunate enough to find a place in a two-story stucco oilfield building a block from downtown. An "oilfield building" means it was the cheapest way to knock things together and plastering the whole mess over with stucco to cover up a lot of bad construction.

It wasn't as easy for us to maintain a Jewish life in Kilgore as it might have been if we lived in Dallas, because we lacked many of the support groups we had in Dallas. There was no schochet to come to our back door to ritually slaughter chickens. There were no friendly "yentas" to sit on the front porch and converse in Yiddish. There were no Jewish bakeries or butcher shops. Had we said, "My background is Jewish," and left it there, life might have been easier, but we were both determined to make a Jewish life for ourselves. When I was in Dallas, I would go to schul with my papa. Had I stayed in Dallas, I would have continued to be a member of my father's schul, the Tifereth Israel, and our life would have remained basically Orthodox.

Here in East Texas, though, we went through the revolution of becoming Reform. I chose to become Reform for one basic reason, and that is that the Orthodox life I grew up with was primarily Yiddish-speaking. Since I was not fluent in Yiddish, large parts of that life were closed to me. When our congregation in Kilgore voted to become Reform and we hired a Reform Rabbi, I began to appreciate my own religion more than I ever had in the past.

When our children came along, they went to Temple with us on Friday night, even if there was a football game or movie they would have to miss. We never regretted leading a Jewish life, and we never regretted telling our neighbors we were Jewish. Even though we live in the Bible Belt, or perhaps because of it, we found that if you respect yourself for who you are, your neighbors will respect you. I don't think our children attended a school in Kilgore where Esther wasn't president of the PTA. She became Kilgore's own "Dear Abby." People trusted and admired her.

I went into the service to serve my country in World War II when I was thirty years old. Every man on the Kilgore faculty had been deferred until the spring semester ended and then we all left at once. We all came back, too! Many Jewish men from Kilgore were serving our country—Nathan Waldman, the Daiches brothers, the Hurwitz brothers, and the Wolfes.

While I was in the service, Esther went home to Dallas to live with her family. I came home on furloughs, and our daughters Madeline (Hartman) and Martha (McDonald) were born in Dallas. I was overseas by the time Martha was born, and like many soldiers, I didn't see my little girl until she was almost a year old. Our son Larry was born Kilgore in 1950, after we had returned to East Texas.

When I came back from the service I worked for the Veteran's Administration in Dallas for one year. I wasn't happy, and I asked Esther, "Are you ready to go home?" She was delighted to hear me say that because she, too, was ready to return to Kilgore.

Our families didn't understand. They said, "You're going to move back to Kilgore? You're going to move away to the country?" But we knew we had a good life here, and we had become part of a good Jewish community in the oilfield.

At first, we had Rabbis that would stay with us a year or two and then move on to larger places. The first Reform Rabbi in Kilgore was Rabbi Simon Cohen, who was learned and wise. I learned so many things from him. He had been in the library at the school in Cincinatti before he came here. Unfortunately, his wife was a harpy. She caused many problems and made his life miserable.

On Friday nights, Francis Gertz would play the piano for services. We would all be seated and getting into the proper frame of mind for a religious service. Just as we were ready to begin, Rabbi Cohen's wife would make her "grand entrance." She would always wait in the back of the room until the services had started, and then she would noisily make her way down the aisle to sit in the first row.

I got a call from the landlord of the small house the Rabbi and his wife rented. He was terribly upset. "I would like you to come and see what Mrs. Cohen has done," he said. I went to the house with him and found that Mrs. Cohen had painted her living room. Now, most landlords would be delighted with a renter who cared enough about the property to make improvements, except that Mrs. Cohen had painted carefully around all the pictures hanging on the walls. She had not removed them, just painted around them and left the old paint underneath.

Rabbi Gerson was a fabulous man. There was also a Rabbi

Gerstein, who was best remembered because he claimed that a horse chased him. He came into the Temple late one Friday night, just huffing and puffing, saying that he was in terrible danger, but I don't think that horse was really interested in him at all.

We were between rabbis when our daughter Madeline was confirmed, so Rabbi Wessel came from Tyler to officiate at the confirmation. He was Rabbi in Tyler for at least fifty years. He was a wonderful man who frequently served area congregations when they were in need of his help.

One of our more noteworthy Rabbis was Rabbi Charles Mantinband, who served Temple Emanu-El in Longview from 1963 until 1971. He was a nationally noted figure. He was Rabbi when our daughter Martha was confirmed.

Most of the Jewish people in Kilgore were about the same age. There was no more than ten years' difference in age from one family to another. Our children grew up together. We always had a good time together. We'd have some kind of activity once every month. We had Sunday school picnics at the park. We had square dancing at the Temple. We had a lot of fun.

Kilgore is a community where the Jewish and Christian citizens are very close. I believe the religious leaders, the rabbis and ministers we have had in this town, have contributed to that closeness.

From the beginning, I have been called upon to speak on Judaism at churches and schools. Abe Gertz and Ben Gertz owned The Toggery, a women's clothing store. Ben Gertz was a wonderful human being. If there ever was a good-hearted individual, it was Ben Gertz. It didn't make any difference if you were Jewish or Christian, if you needed help you went to see Ben Gertz. And if there was any way in this world Ben could help you, whether financially, or with advice, or with kindness, you would get the help you needed.

Hyman Hurwitz was president of the local Chamber of Commerce, and they called him "Mr. Kilgore." I was secretary of the Lion's Club for thirty-eight years. If you honor your friends, they will honor you. I was fortunate to have wonderful friends, both Jews and Christians alike.

By the late fifties, Longview had grown much larger than Kilgore. It had twice as many Jewish families, and they wanted to move the Temple where it would be convenient for the majority. There was some disagreement about building Temple Emanu-El in

Longview. I happen to be among those who did not want to move from Temple Beth Sholom in Kilgore to another place. After all, the beginning was here. It took an awful lot for us to build our Temple. Not only sweat and tears, but heart as well. However, Temple Emanu-El of Longview became the daughter of Temple Beth Sholom of Kilgore. It was the same congregation, the same people, but in a new place.

We were saddened when we were obliged to sell our old Kilgore Temple building, but several thousand dollars remained from the sale. Nathan Waldman and I used the money to purchase a set of the Encyclopedia Judaica and other important Jewish reference books, which we presented to the Kilgore Public library as a living legacy of our community. We made a presentation of money to Temple Emanu-El in Longview. With the remaining money, we went to the Jewish cemeteries in Kilgore and Longview and bought proper markers for the Jewish people who were buried there but did not have headstones.

There was a little short, dried-up man whose name was "Moishe." He was a peddler in the old European style, and he was well known here in the East Texas oilfield. He would go out into the country with a pack on his back, selling clothing, knives and forks, and household things. Moishe left nothing when passed away. There was no one to mourn him or to weep for him, but he was a Jew, and so the Jewish people buried him. He only had a little marker for a headstone, so we replaced it with something permanent.

We also put a stone up in Longview for Henry Feldman, from Overton, who only had a marker and did not have a proper headstone. We feel good about using the money to honor both the living and the dead, as memorials to the present and the past.

The past is always part of the present, and we do well to honor it. My parents came to America from Poland at the end of the nineteenth century. I know practically nothing about their families. I don't know how many uncles and aunts I had, and I never had the chance to meet my cousins. They simply didn't talk about the lives they lived before they came to America. They never wanted to look back. It's difficult to understand how cruel life was for them in Europe and how happy they were to escape to freedom and hope in America.

My mother's name was Lena Waxloch, and she came from

Rodam, where she lived in the ghetto. The ghettos of Europe where Jews were forced to live were nothing like what we now call a ghetto. They had walls and gates that were locked up at night so that people were not allowed to come and go as they pleased. My father, Morris Laufer, came from Lodz, which was the second largest city in Poland.

My parents escaped from Poland in the darkness of night. They first went to London, where my brother was born, but Mama wasn't happy there. Since it was a coal-burning country, the city was covered in soot, and Mama didn't like the darkness or the dirt. They made their way to Capetown, South Africa, but Mama wasn't happy there because the land was so barren. They went across the ocean to Buenos Aires. Mama wasn't happy with Buenos Aires, either, because she didn't feel that Argentina was particularly civilized. Somehow, they found their way to Galveston, Texas, which was a major port of entry to the United States.

The famous Rabbi Henry Cohen of Galveston was responsible for settling more Jewish people in different cities of Texas than any other person in history. He believed it was not wise for Jewish immigrants to congregate in the port of entry as they had done in places like New York City, where opportunities were limited and many of them suffered great hardships. He believed it would be better for people to disperse across the state. Somehow, he managed to find a job for my father with the Sanger brothers, who owned a large retail store in Dallas.

I was born in Dallas, in an area that was once called "North Dallas." It is certainly not the area that is now called "North Dallas." It was actually located right outside what is now downtown. The area had three schuls, an Orthodox schul, a Romanishe (Romanian) schul, and the Tifereth Israel schul, to which my family belonged. They had a mikveh (ritual bath). There was a Jewish bakery and there were Jewish butcher shops. Every Thursday, the schochet (ritual slaughterer) would come to our door with chickens and slaughter them on the spot. By watching him carefully, I learned that the ritual laws required that you kill the animal instantly and humanely, without causing it to suffer.

I was born at the very place where Cleveland intersects with Romaine. Not too many years ago, I tried to find the location and discovered that Cleveland would now meet Romaine right in the center of an interstate highway. So you could say I was born in the middle of an interstate highway!

When I was growing up, the major department stores in Dallas were closed on Rosh Hashanah and Yom Kippur. Sanger Brothers, Neiman-Marcus, Titche-Goettinger, A. Harris, Dreyfus & Sons, all closed. Downtown Dallas was deserted on the High Holy Days. W. A. Green's 5 & 10 cent store was the only store in downtown Dallas that stayed open. They were not Jewish, and there was no reason for them to close, but they didn't do much business because shoppers of every religion stayed home.

I was the only Jewish student at the Travis School on Cedar Springs. When I graduated from elementary school, everyone had a little autograph book to write in. One of the boys wrote in my book and started out, "Dear Jew." That bothered me because it made me feel different, as though I was an outsider in my own world. I don't think it had the same significance and meaning for that little boy as it had for me. Many years later when we came back together for a reunion, he apologized. He said that writing "Dear Jew" in my book had been on his mind all those years and he regretted doing it if it had hurt my feelings. I was able to forgive him, and we both felt better for it.

One of my teachers at Travis encouraged me to continue my violin studies. I played violin with the National High School Orchestra in Wichita, Kansas. I attended North Dallas High School and was the only Jewish student at that school, as well.

To describe how close ties are between the Jews of the East Texas oilfield and those of Dallas and other cities, my religious school teacher was the grandfather of Dr. Ben Andres, who was the first pediatrician in Longview, the great-grandfather of Joyce Andres Stidham of Longview, and the great-great-grandfather of her children, Andrea and Bryan Stidham.

In 1930, my father was working as a salesman for the R&B dress manufacturing company in the old Commerce Building in Downtown Dallas. The R&B Company was owned by the Statman brothers, who brought their young nephew, Joe Statman, to America from Chelm, Poland. My father did everything he could to help Joe learn to speak English and to adjust to a new life in a new country.

Joe was desperately trying to bring his mother, his sister Shayne, his younger brothers Aaron and Charles, Charles' wife Manya and their little son, Irving, into the country. They were all living in Mexico while waiting to qualify to enter this country under the harsh immigration quotas. These immigration quotas were merely cruel anti-Semitic measures designed to keep Jews out.

I remember my father sitting in the front room of our house writing letter after letter to United States senators and congressmen, trying to find a way to help. When they finally came to Dallas, my father helped them learn to speak English. If it wasn't for my father, they would all have spoken like Harvard professors! Once again, in describing what a small world it is, my father was godfather for Charles Statman's younger son, Max, who later made his home in Longview. Max's three children, Charles Barry, Louis Craig, and Sherry Michelle, all grew up in Longview. His oldest son, Charles Barry, is named for his grandfather, who was Joe Statman's brother.

I can only speak about East Texas in positive terms because I had so many positive experiences and met so many wonderful people. I don't think that anything ever happened to me in the oilfield community that's been negative. I have no complaints. Life in the oilfield never dealt me a bad card.

CHAPTER 17

Yom Kippur

by
M. H. Marwil

> I am a Jew in flesh and soul,
> And to this ancient faith I hold
> In trust and duty to transmit
> To generations unborn yet,
> To lives whom I shall never know,
> For as my forebears I shall go.
> A pilgrim on a lonely quest
> To seek at last eternal rest.
>
> But as a Jew my life must be
> Deserving of eternity.
> For every sin I must atone,
> And stand before my God alone,
> Repentant of my sin and blight,
> and humbly pray for Truth and Light,
> That I may better know His way
> And all His holy laws obey.

CHAPTER 18

"Mike" Marwil

"When I heard what was happening, I had to drop what I was doing and go out there to the field to see it for myself. Everybody in town broke their necks to get out there."

There were very few Jewish people living in Henderson, but the Christian community didn't think of the Jewish people as strangers, and the Jewish people didn't think of themselves in that way, either. They were just people and were accepted as part of the community. I think that is demonstrated by the fact that of all N. L. Marwil's children, only their daughter Faye and their oldest son, Moses Marwil, married other Jewish people. The rest all married Christians because that's who they met, that's who they knew and who they were comfortable with.

My father-in-law, N. L. Marwil, was a merchant. He and some other men started the First National Bank. He was a truly community-minded man who did many good things to advance and help the community. He was trustee of the public school for thirty years. He was well thought-of and respected by everyone. One thing he did that shows what kind of a community-minded man he was, when the Baptists needed money to build their new church, my father-in-law loaned them all the money they needed, every bit of it!

His wife, Jeanette, was a Brachfield girl. Although they had lived in Mississippi, her parents, Benjamin and Etta Brachfield, came to Henderson from New Orleans in the 1860s. They had five daughters and only one son. One of the daughters was my husband Leo's mother. One daughter married Mr. Sachse, and another daughter married a Jewish gentleman named Mr. Williams, although that is not a Jewish-sounding name.

Their only son, Charles Brachfield, was an outstanding student and a well-educated man. He was ambitious, but money was scarce when he was a boy. Although his family had enough money to live comfortably, Uncle Charlie thought they shouldn't spend what they had on his education, since he was able to work his way through school. He went to Waco, where he worked at Goldstein-McGill, a ready-to-wear store, and studied law at night. That is not an easy thing to do. As you can imagine, there are not many young men who could accomplish that!

He returned to Henderson after he was admitted to the Texas bar and practiced here all his life. He was county judge in Rusk County from 1898 until 1902 and served as state senator from 1904 until 1908. He was later elected judge of a five-county district. He ran for the Democratic office of attorney general in 1926. He was the first Jewish man to run for statewide office, and he missed the runoff by only 3,600 votes. Although he was defeated in that election, he was successful as a lawyer and businessman. Since he never married and his requirements were few, he built a little penthouse over the First National Bank building and he lived there.

My husband's parents had five sons and only one daughter. Their daughter, Faye, had the whitest complexion, the deepest brown eyes, and the reddest hair. She had so much personality that she seemed to be incredibly beautiful. She was someone very special.

Some people said that Faye was spoiled, although I don't think that was true. Her parents did everything in the world to give her the opportunities a well-educated young lady should have. They even sent her away to finishing school. She learned to play the piano and she went to art school. When she married, she moved away to Corpus Christi, where her husband had a lovely women's clothing store.

Moses Marwil was N. L. and Jeannette Marwil's eldest son. Although he was a brilliant scholar, he only completed one year of college. After he graduated from Henderson High School with honors, he attended Texas A&M, but he was called home to help in his father's store. He never stopped studying, and he had a wonderful education because he was self-educated. When my father-in-law retired, Mose bought out his interest so that he owned the store.

Mose's wife, Stella Jackson, was a Jewish girl from St. Louis. I loved Stella, and Stella loved me. She was a schoolteacher in St. Louis. She was a well-educated young woman with a college degree, which was very rare for young ladies of her generation, but her husband and her children always came first in her life. They always came before any consideration for herself. Stella was one of those ladies who was a "husband worshiper." Stella honestly thought Mose was the most wonderful man, the smartest man, the most perfect man in the world and he could do no wrong. She loved him dearly. He was an obsession with her.

My husband's next-oldest brother, Gus Marwil, went into the army during World War I. Something terrible happened to him in combat, because when he came home he didn't have any ambition. He didn't want to do anything with his life. He lived with his parents. He worked in the store for Mose when Mose needed extra help. He worked in the store full time for a while and he retired early in life.

The middle brother, Bernie, also went into the army in World War I, but he was fortunate enough to be assigned to helping in the kitchen so that he didn't fight in actual combat.

Their brother Harry died of a malignancy when he was only sixteen years old.

My husband Leo was the "baby" of the family, and he always remained very close to his parents. He would drive them wherever they wanted to go, and they went on many nice trips together. He always took them for a drive in their car on Sunday afternoons. Leo also worked for Mose, but when my father-in-law sold the store to Mose and went into the business of buying land, improving it, then selling it for a profit, Leo did the improving of the land.

He was truly ahead of his time. He would have his workmen plant clover and other crops, and then plow them under as nutrients to improve the quality of the land. Although no one else dreamed of keeping mineral rights, he insisted on keeping the mineral rights on any land they sold. Geologists had been in East Texas off and on during those years. They would drill a well and be disappointed with it and leave, telling everyone that there was no oil here. When the oil boom finally came, we were better off because of those mineral rights.

C. M. "Dad" Joiner was in Rusk County in those early days. His son John Joiner and John's wife were here also. I can remember how they had to skimp and scrape to make ends meet so that they could stay in Henderson, but they were determined to stick it out. They worked terribly hard. We would listen to John Joiner and his wife say, "There's definitely oil under this ground." Most of us paid little attention because we thought they were dreamers. When oil finally came in, it was a big surprise to everyone, but not to them.

The first thing I remember about the oil boom was that my husband was the happiest man in the world. He helped his father in those real estate transactions, and it was through him that they had those mineral rights. You see, oil hit here in 1929, when there were bread lines all over the United States. Because of the oil boom, Henderson never had a bread line. We never had that kind of poverty. We escaped the worst of the Great Depression, which was so horrible for the rest of the nation.

That first well, the Daisy Bradford #3 at Joinerville, came in as a gusher. There was such excitement in this town! When I heard what was happening, I had to drop what I was doing and go out there to the field to see it for myself. I wasn't alone. Everybody in town broke their necks to get out there. The earth rumbled and shook like you wouldn't believe it, and before you knew what was happening, black oil was shooting up as high as the derrick. It came out with a lot of force. The people were beside themselves! They got right out there and wallowed in the oil!

People swarmed into this area like bees swarming to a beehive. New merchants came from everywhere. Businesses sprang up overnight. We had two hotels in our little town, but that was certainly not enough room for everyone. Two- and three-room shacks were brought in and dumped here and there.

Longview wasn't much of a town then, and Kilgore wasn't anything at all, so the richer people would settle their families in Tyler, which was an older and more stable town, and they would commute back and forth to the oilfield.

My husband Leo decided he could make more money by being a notary public and working with the oilmen. They were leasing property everywhere, and Leo knew the local people. He went out with the oilmen, the "lease hounds," to notarize papers right on the spot. He made himself unpopular lots of times, but he saw to it that no one was taken advantage of when he was there. He would say, "Do you understand this?" and he would be sure to explain what it was all about. Maybe the lease hounds didn't lie about things, but they never explained them too deeply, either. That's why Leo would insist on explaining the papers before people would sign. He worked by the day, and he got the unheard-of salary of $20 a day!

A boom town is different from anything else you can imagine, and the boom changed a lot of people who may not have been strong to begin with. Some had more money than common sense, and there were quite a few divorces. But for the most part, people were grateful for their good fortune. They realized that there was poverty everywhere else, but not in East Texas. Some of the people went berserk

Bringing in the Daisy Bradford #3. Mike Marwil said, "Everybody in town broke their necks to get out there."

—Texas Mid Continent Oil & Gas Association Photo

and did silly things, but other people were able to educate their children and do things for their families that they had never dared to dream of doing. There wasn't much to do for entertainment. We only had one little picture show, but it didn't even open on Sundays.

I don't know whether I changed any or not because of the oil boom, but I don't think I did. I was growing into young womanhood. I kept the boy I was in love with and couldn't get interested in anyone else. He was the foundation for my life. You might say that he was the plot of ground on which I pitched my tent.

I was raised as an Episcopalian. My grandfather and his brother came to Overton, Texas, on horseback as part of a covered wagon caravan. Our family name was Bailey. When I was a child, my daddy used to tell me I was related to Molly Bailey, the famous Texas circus queen. As a little girl, I cherished the idea of being related to someone so elegant and glamorous as the circus queen!

My family came to Henderson, where I met the boy who would become my husband. Leo had seen me and asked his friends, his acquaintances, and anybody he knew if they would introduce us. But the other boys only teased him and wouldn't do it, so he knew that he had to take matters into his own hands. One Sunday morning, he saw me sitting on the porch of my house as he was driving past. He stopped his car, walked right up, and introduced himself. He said, "I hope you won't think I'm being forward. I have to find someone to introduce us properly, but I have not been able to do so, and I would like to get to know you."

That was the start of our long romance, although we waited until rather late in life to marry. My husband's mother did not want him to marry out of his faith. She didn't mean any unkindness to me. She liked me as a person, and I loved her. She often invited me to the house for meals. She would always invite me to come along when Leo took them for their Sunday-afternoon drive in their big Cadillac limousine. She taught me how to do a lot of things, but she always told me, "If you and my son marry, life will be difficult for both of you."

In spite of it all, we were friends. Deep down, I knew she loved me, but she thought that if her son married out of his faith he would never be Jewish again. Out of respect for his mother, we waited until she died before we married. Leo's mother died of a malignancy in 1934, and we married in 1935.

Even though we respected her enough to wait until she was gone before we married, we both knew that she was mistaken. Leo always remained Jewish. Although I attended services with him many times, Leo never came to church with me. He wasn't familiar with the ritual of the Episcopal Church, and I wouldn't ever ask him to do anything that would make him uncomfortable.

After we married, we came to live in the big house with my father-in-law. Papa would tell me what he would like to eat. I didn't do the cooking because he had a cook, but I would tell her what to prepare and then I would go into the kitchen and bake. The cook didn't bake, and I always liked bakery foods. We lived with Papa until he decided he was lonely and he wanted to marry. He married an aunt of Stella's who had visited Henderson off and on when Leo's mother was living. Stella's aunt Nettie was in her early fifties. My father-in-law was much older than she was, but he was very active. I don't know how old Papa was, but Leo was his baby boy, and Leo was in his early forties at that time.

Leo and I moved into a home of our own when Papa and Aunt Nettie married. When Papa died, he willed the big family home to Leo, and so we came back to live in it. Aunt Nettie moved to an apartment in Shreveport. She later lived in a nursing home in Longview until she died.

There was once a misunderstanding about the rabbi in Tyler. We liked the Tyler people, and of course they had nothing to do with it. Like all denominations, once in a while you find a leader who doesn't belong in the clergy, and the rabbi they had at the time was one of those people.

The little Williams boy died tragically. The family made all the arrangements and carried the boy's body to Tyler for the funeral. Moments before the funeral was to begin, the rabbi called my father-in-law to the side and asked what there was "in it" for him: how much money he would receive for performing the funeral. It made my father-in-law so angry that he said, "There's nothing in it for you because I'm not going to use you." Papa turned to Uncle Charlie, Judge Brachfield, and asked him to conduct the poor little boy's funeral services. That is why the family never went to Tyler again.

When the rabbi in Palestine heard what had happened, he came by and apologized for the other man and did what he could to comfort the family. He invited the family to attend services with his congregation, Temple Beth Israel, which met in private homes in Palestine. Some of the family went to worship with the people in Palestine for a while. We never had a Temple in Henderson. The Jewish people here observed the holidays in their homes. We would often go to Kilgore or Shreveport for services, and in later years my husband and I would go to Longview.

The oil boom changed a lot of things, but it didn't change us all that much.

CHAPTER 19

S. M. (Mendy) Rabicoff

"Growing up in Kilgore was a different experience from in other places, because Kilgore was a much wilder town than anything you can imagine."

My grandfather, Harry Sobol, came to Kilgore from Oklahoma as soon as the oil boom hit in 1930. He rented a building from the Wilson Supply Company and brought an employee down from Oklahoma to work with him, but the man didn't stay. The man simply didn't like living in the wild oilfield town. He didn't care for the whiskey, the prostitutes, and the shootings, and he couldn't imagine bringing his family to such a terrible place. That was no problem for my grandfather, because my grandmother remained in Seminole, Oklahoma, to run their business there.

My parents, Sarah and Smiley Rabicoff, had been married five or six years at that time. My father made a lot of money in St. Joseph, Missiouri, during Prohibition. Along with the making and selling alcohol, he owned a gambling parlor, a cigar store, and other businesses, but the day Prohibition was repealed he found himself suddenly out of business.

My grandfather called him from Kilgore and said, "There's a good opportunity to make a living down here in the Texas oilfield," but my dad told him that he didn't know anything about oil or the oilfield.

My grandfather said, "You don't need to know anything. This is how it works: You buy something, you sell it for a profit. You trade what you can trade. Anyone can do it."

So my dad came to Kilgore to see what he could buy and sell or trade. After a month, he was ready to return to St. Jo. My dad was accustomed to having other people work for him, and to working whenever he wanted to work. During the oil boom, business in Kilgore was a twenty-four-hour, seven-day-a-week job. The long hours and hard work were only part of his problems. The other problem was that he agreed with my grandfather's former employee. He didn't think this was a fit place to live. This wild oilfield town was not exactly what you dreamed of as the ideal place to bring your wife and raise your family. My grandfather encouraged him to stay, and Mama followed him here with my sisters, Jackie and Shirley, who were still babies.

At first, they all lived in a little apartment behind the store. The first thing Daddy did was add another room to the building for Shirley and Jackie. When I was born in 1940, he added another room for me.

The Sobol family in Oklahoma in 1937. L-R, standing: Meyer Sobol, Marie Sobol, Harry Sobol, Pauline Lumel, Max Lumel, three unknown people; sitting: Hack Sobol, Harry Pollack, Sarah Sobol Rabicoff, Gus Sobol (later Leaman), Jene Sobol Krasner, Sam Krasner.

—Photo courtesy Jackie Cooper

A year after they arrived, my dad bought the business from Grandpa, but Grandpa's name, Sobol, was on the sign. Since it was a perfectly good sign, they didn't see any reason to change it, and neither do I. The business remains Sobol to this day.

I was fourteen years old when Grandpa died. The last two years of his life, he lived in our house and shared my bedroom. He was old, but he used to tell me the most amazing stories.

He told me how he came to the United States from the shores of the Black Sea. Although the area is now part of Romania, it was Russia when he left. The word "sobol" means furrier. This could indicate that his family might have been fur traders in the old country.

He was the only member of his family who came to America through Ellis Island. The rest of his family went to Mexico City and came to the United States through Galveston. Some of them stayed in Mexico City and are third-generation Mexicans now.

He wasn't happy in New York. He had a relative in St. Louis, so he went there. The relative advised him to go to Fort Smith, Arkansas. In Fort Smith, he met Samuel Pollock from Talihina, a community about forty miles across the border into Oklahoma. He later married Samuel Pollock's daughter, Marie.

My great-grandfather, Samuel Pollock, had settled in Talihina, in the Indian Territory in the 1860s and built a general store where he sold a little bit of everything. He told my grandfather he could make a good living by going out into the countryside and selling bolts of fabric, pots and pans, and other goods to the Indians. My grandfather started going to Talihina from Fort Smith. Then he branched out into other places like Wewoka and Seminole.

He went out to the Indian Territory to find out what the Indians wanted and needed. The Indians didn't have any metal pots and pans, and they didn't have any good sharp knives. They wanted any kind of woven cloth. They had corn and corn meal, but they wanted wheat flour. He went back to Fort Smith to buy those things and returned to sell them. Although the Indians did have gold coins, for the most part, business was conducted through a barter system. He would trade pots and pans and cloth for whatever they had to trade. He might trade two or three bags of corn for one piece of hand-woven cloth, or trade a pot for ten pieces of Indian pottery, or blankets or pelts.

His way of doing business may not make a lot of sense to us in today's age. It took four or five days to get out to where the Indians lived and four or five days to come back to what we might call "civilization," and he didn't have any idea of what he would do with the Indians' goods once he got back to Fort Smith.

Although roads were primitive and didn't have route numbers, they had markers, just like we have now. A man might travel to Talihina on the "blue" road, which had blue markers on the rocks and trees, or he might go somewhere on the "red" road, where the markers were in red. It was a simple system, but it worked.

My grandfather would sell stuff to one group of Indians, and they would turn around and sell it to other groups of Indians to make a profit. Many of the Indians he dealt with stayed in one location, so they were able to sell things to the Indians who moved around all the time.

All this took place in McCurtain County north of Talihina. Can you imagine this young Jewish man, fresh from the shores of the Black Sea, all alone in the middle of the Oklahoma Indian Territory? It's interesting to wonder what the he thought when he first saw the Indians. It's just as interesting to wonder what the Indians thought when they first saw him. The Indians figured all white people looked pretty much alike, and he figured all non-Jews looked pretty much alike, so nobody thought anything was that unusual. Grandpa didn't speak much English, but then, neither did the Indians, so that wasn't a problem. They got along remarkably well even though they couldn't speak the same language. They could somehow manage to communicate with a few words, with hand signals and pantomime.

The Indians took a liking to him. When he arrived in their village they would honor him with a big meal. They would always fix a special kind of roast meat for him, and he liked it very much. He would ask them what it was and they would tell him it was "paw-nay." There was no such word as "paw-nay" in Russian or in Yiddish, and so he had no idea of what he was eating, but he kept asking. Finally, his hosts took him to the corral and pointed to a small horse. "Paw-nay," they said, "paw-nay." He realized he had been eating pony, horse meat! Of course, he was horrified, but he'd been eating it all those months and he didn't want to offend the people who had been so gracious to him, so he kept right on eating it.

Near the turn of the century, Grandpa decided to settle down and build a store in Seminole, Oklahoma. It was the post office and general store. He sold a little bit of everything, from cloth to clothing, from household supplies to ice, from food to caskets. My grandmother, Marie, helped in the store and took care of their eight children. One child died, so she ended up raising seven. Her life must have been hard, but she was accustomed to a hard life on the frontier. She grew up in her father's general store in Talihina.

My great-grandfather, Samuel Pollock, ran off with an Indian woman. He left his four daughters and his thirteen-year-old son, my Uncle Harry, with the business and all the money and he disappeared into the Indian Territory. He showed up once, about twenty years later, for Thanksgiving dinner. After dinner he disappeared and that was the last they heard of him.

Uncle Charlie was Harry Sobol's uncle and my great-great uncle. When he was thirty-five years old, he moved to Seminole. Somehow, Uncle Charlie had two wives and three daughters. I don't know exactly how he managed to have two wives at the same time, but they were two respectable Jewish women from Russia and they all got along just fine.

Remember, this was frontier in the 1890s. Life was not like we know it today. There was no electricity. There was no running water, no indoor plumbing. These people spoke Russian and Yiddish and they were living in the midst of a bunch of Indians who didn't speak either Russian or Yiddish, or English for that matter. Possibly one of the women was widowed or abandoned and Uncle Charlie took her in? I don't know. There were no telephones, so she couldn't call her family back home. There were no planes or trains, so she couldn't pick up and leave. It would have been difficult for a woman to be abandoned in that rough territory. They may have decided it was better to be Charlie Sobol's extra wife than to be alone in the Indian Territory.

Uncle Charlie came down with some disease so that he couldn't work to support himself and his unusual family. My grandpa felt it was his responsibility to look after them, so they all moved into his house. There were few doctors and little medical attention on the frontier. Whatever Uncle Charlie came down with proved to be fatal. Uncle Charlie died in July. My grandfather felt it was his responsibility to see that Uncle Charlie had a proper Jewish burial. Unfortunately, the nearest Jewish cemetery was in Dallas, several hundred miles away.

There they were, in Oklahoma at the turn of the last century, with no easy way to carry the body to Dallas for a proper Jewish burial. My grandfather sold ice in his store. It was brought down from Canada and stored in sawdust containers. Grandpa put Uncle Charlie in the wagon, wrapped him in a tarpaulin, filled it full of ice, and covered it with straw to keep him from smelling. Then Grandpa took an Indian friend with him to help him drive the wagon, and off they went to Dallas.

After the long, hard journey, they took Uncle Charlie to the Shearith Israel Cemetery in Dallas, where many members of our family are now buried. My great-great-grandfather, who was Samuel Pollock's father, was buried there in 1852. Grandpa and his Indian friend unloaded the body from the wagon, but the people at the Shearith Israel told him they wanted five hundred dollars to bury Uncle Charlie. Five hundred dollars! A major fortune in those days.

Grandpa said, "Where am I going to get five hundred dollars? All I've got is fifty dollars. I'll give you the fifty dollars and I'm leaving." With that, he climbed back into the wagon and started to leave. They said, "Stop! Wait! Where are you going?" Grandpa told them, "Do what you want to do. He's a Jew, and you are required by Jewish law to bury him. I've done my part to get him to a Jewish cemetery where he can have a proper Jewish burial. I can't afford five hundred dollars. Take the fifty dollars, or you get nothing and you still have to bury him!"

So they agreed to bury Uncle Charlie for fifty dollars. Then Grandpa went back to Oklahoma. Knowing my grandfather, as long as he had an empty wagon anyhow, I'm sure he stopped in Dallas to buy whiskey and goods to take back and sell.

Uncle Charlie's two wives also died. The oldest daughter stayed with my grandparents and worked in Grandfather's store, but my grandfather didn't feel that he was able to raise Uncle Charlie's other two daughters. He sent them to a Jewish orphanage in New Orleans. He always kept in touch with them, and a little later he had the two girls transferred to a Jewish orphanage in Houston.

Several years ago, my daughters Ana and Smila were visiting their grandparents, Obbie and Edith Lewis, in Houston. My mother-in-law had arranged for Smila to play with the young niece of a friend who was visiting from Laredo. The name Sobol came up in the conversation and the girl said, "That was my great-grandmother's name." Although the families had been separated for years, the little girls discovered they were cousins! The little girl was the grand-daughter of one of Uncle Charlie's daughters who had been sent away to the orphanage!

Although they were still living in Seminole, my grandparents happened to be visiting in Fort Towson near Broken Bow when my mother was born. So they opened a store there. In 1912 or 1913, oil was discovered in a little town with an Indian name, about six-teen or seventeen miles west of Broken Bow. As he had done be-fore, my grandfather hurried right over to see what he could bring in to sell.

Since he had a post office in his store in Seminole, he agreed to try to get a post office for the little town with the Indian name. Somewhere between the time he left and the time he got on the train to go to Washington, he forgot the name the town had decided to call itself. The Post Office Department in Washington had to have a name right then and there. He didn't know what else to do, so he told them the name of the town was Sobol, Oklahoma. If you ever go to Oklahoma, go to Broken Bow, take a left, and after about fifteen miles you will come to Sobol, Oklahoma. They have a general store, a Baptist church and the Sobol School. It's one of two towns in the state of Oklahoma that's named after a Jew.

The only Jewish life in Seminole was that every Friday night my grandfather held his five-minute religious service and the children all had Sunday school. Their Sunday school was held in one of the store rooms of my grandfather's store, and it was taught with books my grandfather brought from Fort Smith or St. Louis. Sunday school was self-taught from those books, except for what my grandfather knew. Although all their children were raised outside of what you would call the "mainstream" of American Judaism, they did what they could to bring them up to respect and honor their religion. All the children married Jewish people and continued to lead Jewish lives and to build Jewish homes.

To show what a small world the oil patch is, my mother was Sunday school teacher for Sarah Picow and Milton Galoob when they were children in Seminole, and they all wound up living in the Longview and Kilgore area.

I never met my father's parents. They died before I was born, and I only knew them through photographs. My grandfather was a very small man. My father was five feet nine inches tall, and his father was four or five inches shorter.

My grandmother was very blond and fair, like my daughter Smila and me. My father's parents had also come to America from Russia. It was necessary for my grandfather to escape from Russia because even though he was married and had a small child, the Russians were going to take him into the army. In those days, going into the Russian army was the same as a death sentence for a Jewish boy. Few of them survived. Since everybody from their area went to St. Joseph, Missouri, that's where my father and his family went.

My father was only a year old when they came to this country. He got his unusual name, "Smiley," when the family arrived at Ellis Island. He was a happy, smiling baby, so the immigration officials called him "Smiley." Most likely, their last name was originally spelled "Ribicoff," not "Rabicoff."

They were desperately poor, and they lived a desperate life. My grandfather started walking up and down the streets with a sack on his back, picking up pieces of scrap metal and selling them for whatever he could get. Later, he was able to get a pushcart. Much later, when my daddy was twelve or thirteen years old, he bought my grandfather a horse to pull the cart and, as you can imagine, that was his big moment of glory.

My father, Smiley Rabicoff, only had a fourth-grade education. He was intelligent, and he would have liked to have had a better education, but that was not his fate. My grandfather suffered from some form of respiratory disease so that he was unable to work regularly. When my father was seven or eight years old, he had to leave school so he could go to work selling newspapers to support his family any way he could. He was the oldest of eleven children; that was what was expected of him. They made do. They survived. He was self-educated, but he respected education and he sent his younger brothers to college.

None of these people ever talked about life in Europe. It was as though their lives started the day they came to America. America was everything to them. Although my father's parents couldn't speak English, they expected him to always speak English. They would speak to him in Yiddish, but they demanded that he answer them in English. They said, "English is the language of America and you have to speak English."

When my family came to Kilgore for the oil boom, they found a number of other Jewish people in this wild town. People always want to know how the Jewish people of Kilgore located each other. Well, my daddy would drive down the street and look at the new signs that were put up above the stores. Daiches, Ettelman, Hurwitz. He saw Sam Goldman's clothing store and said, "Sam Goldman? The guy's got to be Jewish." So he went into the store to introduce himself and yes, Sam Goldman was Jewish.

If you look at old photographs of downtown Kilgore, you can see the signs with all the Jewish names on them. These days you would leaf through a phone book to do the same thing, but back then they just looked at the signs to find each other.

They got their little group together to hold Friday-night religious services at somebody's house and share social fellowship as well. They might eat dinner or play cards and talk.

In addition to the families living in Kilgore, Overton had fifteen or twenty Jewish families, including my mother's cousin Dr. Heiligman and his wife and family. All these children needed a religious education, so they went back to the same self-taught pattern they knew in Oklahoma. Daddy had religious books brought in from St. Jo., Missouri. They started meeting at our store or at Sam Goldman's store to hold Sunday school classes.

After meeting informally for several years, the people eventually decided to build a Temple. The Congregation was called Congregation Beth Sholom. When you're a little kid, a Temple seems like the biggest building in the world, but Temple Beth Sholom was not very big. The pulpit was at the back of the sanctuary. Behind the pulpit there were two little rooms on either side and one little bitty narrow room across the back where Sunday school was held. It wasn't even big enough to accommodate all the children. Kids were coming from Longview, Kilgore, Gladewater, Henderson, Overton, and outlying areas. We had thirty-five or forty children in Sunday school and we had no room, so they set about finding some economical way to make the building larger. Hymie Hurwitz located an old beer joint. They sawed it in half and brought it to the Temple location. It had one set of little rooms down the whole side of the building. I don't even want to speculate on what those rooms were originally used for, but they became our Sunday school rooms.

The Temple owned the lot where the original building was built, but Mr. Leggett Crim owned the other two lots where they put the social hall. Hymie Hurwitz offered to buy the land, but Mr. Crim said, "I will let you use it as long as you want it." The land was put down on the tax rolls as being used for religious purposes and tax was never charged on it.

My grandfather talked Sam Roosth of Tyler into donating the memorial plaque for the Temple. Sam Roosth was in the oil business. Henry Feldman and Bill Goldman were in the pipe business. They would all do business together, and Sam would often come from Tyler to Kilgore to attend services. One day, he came into the building and looked around and told my grandfather, "This cannot be a schul, because you don't have a memorial plaque. You're not doing anything in memory of the people who've died."

My grandfather said, "If you're such a good Jew, why don't you buy a memorial plaque and donate it?" So that's how my grandfather talked Sam Roosth into donating the memorial plaque, which is now located at Temple Emanu-El in Longview.

Originally, the synagogue was Conservative but at some point they decided to become Reform. When I was a little kid, the men always wore black yamalkas (skull caps) and tallesim (prayer shawls.) When the congregation became Reform, the same people stayed, but the yamalkas and talesim were piled up outside the sanctuary and nobody used them anymore.

I enjoyed growing up in Kilgore. I had a good childhood. I liked all the Jewish holidays and social activities. There were covered-dish suppers and bingo games. There were the all-day Sunday school picnics where the parents and children had a good time. At every holiday, the kids put on a play of some sort. No matter what the occasion, there was always a play. At Purim, I always played the part of the villain, Haman. I was Haman until I was fourteen years old!

Sometimes we had as many as twenty-five young people in our youth group. That may not seem big for a metropolitan congregation, but that was big for Kilgore. We shared activities with the kids in Shreveport and Tyler. The youth group went to conclaves in San Antonio, Houston, or Fort Worth. It was a big deal to go to Echo Hill Camp in Kerrville every year.

When I was twelve years old, I was driving my car. Everybody in Kilgore drove early. You got your license when you were fourteen. When I was fourteen years old, I was a member of an A.Z.A. group in Dallas. Charles Hurwitz, David Andres, and I would drive to Dallas two or three times a month. I had my own car. The kids we ran around with in Dallas couldn't believe it! They normally didn't get a car until they graduated from high school.

We would drive to Dallas and we would stay with my uncle and aunt, Sam and Jene Krasner. Jene was my mother's sister. Sam was rich. They lived in a big two-story home in old Preston Hollow, with food and fun and people in and out all the time. We always stayed in the servants' quarters, where we had privacy and could do as we liked, come and go as we liked.

The kids who grew up in Dallas may have had a more intense Jewish experience because there were more Jewish kids for them to associate with. In Kilgore, we associated with everybody. I had a lot of Christian friends. I never even heard about anti-Semitism. We never felt "different," we were just some of the kids in town. I don't know if it was because of the healthy relationships our parents had with the rest of the community, or because we lived in a truly good community.

During the summer months, my dad and mother had monthly fish fries at which there were Jewish and Christian families together. It didn't matter. All the kids in Kilgore were always together.

Growing up in Kilgore was different from in other places because until 1960, Kilgore was a much wilder town than anything you can imagine. It was the first wet town coming from the west and from the south, so people from Tyler, Henderson, Nacogdoches, and Lufkin were always coming to Kilgore for a drink. The population of Kilgore grew by leaps and bounds every Friday night. That was true in all the beer joints around the outskirts of town. Kids came from other places because they could buy alcohol in Kilgore that they couldn't buy at home.

We had a lake house. We had boats. The Dallas kids came to visit us for the weekends and holidays. My relatives from Colorado, Kansas City, and from Mexico City would send their kids to us for two or three weeks or a month in the summertime.

We grew up quicker than they did because of the cars and money. Everything was available to us. We had real mobility from a very early age and they didn't. They had to stay in groups because they had no other means of transportation. If we went to a conclave in San Antonio when we were teenagers, Charles and I would get into the car and drive there. If we wanted to get a beer and go dancing, we could get into the car and go to the beer joints and go dancing. If we wanted to go shoot dice, we could go to any number of places and do that, or go shoot pool for money, or play the roulette wheel in the building behind the Brass Rail, downtown. You could do anything you wanted to do in Kilgore. It was a lot like Galveston. It was a wide-open town.

When I was sixteen years old, three or four of us would drive to Mexico. It was nothing for me to pick up the phone and call a girl in Dallas on Friday afternoon, drive up there Friday night, take her out on a date, and turn around and come home. As a result, kids my own age seemed childish to me. When I was a senior in high school, I was dating a Tri-Delt Junior at the University of Texas. During the fall I would go to Austin for parties. Most of the girls I dated were two or three years older than I was, except for Natalie, the girl I married.

I attended Kilgore College, and then I went to Oklahoma University for a couple of days before Rush started because I planned to go to college there. I was staying at the Sammy fraternity house until my apartment was ready. I had already attended Kilgore College, so I was a little older than the boys at the fraternity house. Their big deal for an evening was to put their nickels and dimes together to buy a pizza and a pitcher of beer and sit around drinking.

My idea of spending an evening was to take a girl to dinner or go dancing. I didn't spend the whole night sitting around with a bunch of guys over one pizza and one pitcher of beer. I didn't fit in with them, so I left and went to the University of Houston. They did the same things in Houston. I felt as though they were a bunch of kids. None of them had cars. Their parents either couldn't or didn't give them any money to spend.

I was staying at the Phi Epsilon Pi Fraternity house at the University of Houston, and the fraternity brothers wanted to get me a blind date. Natalie had been one of five high school girls who had been asked to run for their fraternity sweetheart, so they showed me her photograph in their fraternity sweetheart book. That was it. I took her out. We were married three and a half years later in Fort Smith, Arkansas. We have two daughters, Ana and Smila, and the sign over our business still says "Sobol" because it still a perfectly good sign and there is no reason to change.

CHAPTER 20

Vera Remer

"The old-timers considered the oilfield people roughnecks and riff-raff and would not have much to do with them."

My family came to East Texas long before the oil boom. My great-grandfather, Benjamin Brachfield, and my grandmother Etta came to Henderson from Vicksburg, Mississippi, in the early 1870s. They had six children. One of them was my grandmother, Jeannette Brachfield Marwilsky.

My other grandfather, Nathan L. Marwilsky, was born in Poland. He made his way to the United States and came to Henderson in the 1880s. He wasn't very tall and he was very slender, but he and my grandmother had a great big family of boys and they were all scared to death of him.

When he first came to Henderson, my grandfather opened a saloon, but after he married and had children he didn't want his children to grow up in the questionable atmosphere of a saloon. It was a good business but it wasn't "nice," so he sold the saloon and went into the grocery business. Grandfather didn't carry fancy or elegant merchandise because he sold mostly to the local farmers. He was the first to bring lettuce and ice to Henderson. Back then the diet in rural areas was very limited. They had lots of turnip greens, but they had never seen lettuce. It was a great delicacy. Since they never had any ice at all, that was a wonderful novelty and a real treat. The farmers would come into town twice a year and run up a big bill on credit. It was understood that they couldn't pay until their crops came in. My grandfather always advanced his customers what they needed and shouldered the responsibility until they were able to pay him.

From the grocery business, Grandfather went into the retail business and opened a dry goods store on the town square. Henderson had a rectangular square with the Rusk County Courthouse at one end of it. When they originally planned the town they intended to put the courthouse in the middle of the square, but they forgot to leave enough room for it, so they had to put it at the end. Years later, they tore the courthouse down, and in its place they put up a statue of General Rusk, for whom Rusk County is named.

My grandparents had five sons and one daughter. My father, Moses Marwil, was the eldest son. His brothers were Gus, Bernard, Harry, and Leo, and his sister was Faye. People used to say that the daughter got all the looks in the family, and I suppose that was a good thing for Aunt Faye. Since she was the only girl, she was rather spoiled. She learned to play the piano, and they even sent her away to finishing school! My father graduated from high school as valedictorian of his class in 1901, before he was sixteen years old. They said that he won all the honors, but they gave him the one significant honor of being valedictorian. He attended Texas A&M College for one semester, but Grandfather needed his help, so he returned to Henderson and went to work in the family store.

My grandfather and my grandmother's brother, Judge Charles L. Brachfield, along with several other old-timers, founded the First National Bank in Henderson.

My father was always an outgoing person, so it became his job to go to market in St. Louis to buy merchandise for the store. He met my mother while he was in St. Louis. Her name was Stella Jackson, and she was a schoolteacher. They were married in St. Louis in 1913 and went to New Orleans on their honeymoon.

When Father proposed to Mother, he promised her that after living in Henderson for a year they would move to the big city of Dallas. It must have been a shock to Mother, who had grown up in the metropolitan surroundings of St. Louis, to find herself living in a small, dusty East Texas town that had no paved streets or sidewalks.

After my father and mother married, he bought out my grandfather's interest in the retail business. Father always said he would rather be a "big fish in a little pond," and Mother never had the heart to enforce his promise to move away. That one year stretched to almost fifty, and our parents were still living in the same house that father had built for mother as a bride. My father shortened his name from Marwilsky to Marwil before he was married because he didn't want his children to go through life with a name that was difficult to pronounce. My grandfather shortened his name at the same time since it was easier for him to have the same name as his son, both for business and legal reasons. Everyone in Henderson knew Papa's family, and of course they all knew that we were Jewish, which was not the reason for changing the name. It was simply a convenience.

Henderson was a crossroads. Even today there are many highways leading to Henderson. There were many Jewish families who lived in Henderson at one time or another, long before the East Texas oil boom, who either moved away or died. It's been so long ago I can't even remember their names.

When the oil boom hit in 1930, business was so good that the stores had to stay open from early in the morning until late at night to serve the people who came flocking into town. Suddenly, we had many more stores and many more people and all that newfound money. Although Henderson was not quite as overcrowded as Kilgore and Longview, we were very crowded. Anyone who had an extra room or any kind of space to spare would rent it to strangers so that all the rooms were immediately taken. The streets were filled with people, but they weren't the sort of people you would want to associate with. They were rough. The old-timers considered the oil-field people to be roughnecks and riff-raff and would not have much to do with them. The banks certainly weren't going to lend money for that sort of "irresponsible thing."

Some people named Packman came in with the boom. They opened a dry goods store which sold a higher grade of merchandise than my father's store did. Another family, named Hartholtz, also came with the boom. They had one son. The lady's name was Esther Hartholtz, and my mother played bridge with her. K. Wolens was originally in Corsicana, but at one time they had a store in Henderson. There was also a Jewish family name Endel who had a store and became very competitive. Every time Papa would dress his windows, they would dress their windows exactly the same way.

The oil boom offered our town a lot of opportunities it wouldn't have had otherwise, but many of the old-timers were happy with things the way they were and couldn't see any reason for change.

The oil boom made some people immensely wealthy in spite of themselves. People went from being dirt poor to having all the money in the world. Some behaved strangely because they didn't know what to do with so much newfound money. Some had their money spent before they even received it! Some went wild and did outrageous things. Others kept their good sense and didn't let the oil money change them.

Many of the black farmers were "skinned" out of their oil rights by disreputable oilmen who would come to their farms and say, "I'll give you two or three hundred dollars for your farm." That sounded like big money back then. It was more money than they had ever seen or ever hoped to see. A few may have been smart enough to keep the oil rights, but sadly enough, the majority of them had it stolen right out from under them.

We had three theaters in town during the oil boom. There were two or three drugstores where people would congregate to meet each other and socialize. Jay's Cafe downtown did a land-office business. Their food was wonderful! People came from miles around to eat there, and you had to wait a long time for a table. The tables were like little booths with curtains you could draw if you wanted privacy. They served excellent light rolls which they brought and kept on bringing. The minute a roll got cool enough that you could pick it up in your hand, a waiter would come and give you another hot roll. They gave you a lot of food, and it was good.

There were dances at Mattie's Ballroom in Gregg County. Although our East Texas roads were bad, they weren't bad enough to keep people from going to Mattie's Ballroom.

The oil boom didn't have that much effect on me. Children's lives were different from what they are today. We were expected to behave ourselves. We ate and slept and went to school. Some children in town were allowed to go to the drugstore after school, but we were always expected to go directly home. We were not nearly as well in-formed as children are today. We had no television of course, but our parents bought a set of the World Book Encyclopedia for us. We read the encyclopedia, and we had contests at the dinner table to see which child could recall the most information about an assigned section. We were encouraged to read extensively.

When I was ten years old, the three of us children were sent to visit my grandmother's house. After we had been there for a while, the phone rang. I remember Grandmother taking the phone off the hook, then turned around to us and said, "You have a new little baby sister at home."

That's the first I heard about it, and all I could think was, "Oh, no, more crying." I didn't even know my mother was pregnant. Ladies didn't believe it was proper to discuss such things with children. Heavens, no! Now the mothers will even let the children feel the baby kick and they will tell them all about it, but in those days it was a carefully kept secret.

It was fun to grow up in a small southern town where you knew everyone. I have two sisters and one brother. I'm the oldest. My sister Doris Frost is next. My sister Shirley Sanger was a member of the famous Rangerette drill team at Kilgore College and is still a member of the "Rangerettes Forever" organization. She lives in Dallas, where she became active in many groups and organizations. My brother, Stanley Marwil, the "brains" of our family, retired from Phillips Petroleum in Bartlesville, Oklahoma.

When we were growing up, we were the only Jewish children in town, except for our cousins the Wolfes. But they lived in and out of Henderson, in Houston and other places. Their mother was also a Brachman girl. She was a sister to my grandmother.

When we were small we didn't feel "different" from any of our classmates. We never realized there was a difference until the day a neighbor boy called us "Jew baby!" It was our first awareness that prejudice existed in the world. After that, being the only Jewish children in town wasn't as easy for us. We didn't suffer physical harm, but the others let us know that we were "different." We were often quite isolated because we were "the Jews."

When we became teenagers, we would visit the young people's groups at the churches or we would be all by ourselves, and it's not healthy for teenagers to be all by themselves. I don't think it was as hard for my brother and sisters as it was for me, because I was a shy child. It was easier for me to spend my life with the people I met in books than with real people. My sister Doris insists that she remembers my mother calling me to do chores and I would answer, "I can't come right now, I'm reading a book!" That excuse didn't "hold water" with Mother, who prized obedience and industriousness as well as scholarship.

My sister Shirley was a tennis player in high school. My sister Doris was on the high school debate team. We all went to high school football games, even though we didn't have a football stadium in Henderson, only an open field. It was awfully hard to tell how many yards the team made, because the yards were only marked off with chalk lines on the field. You had to trust the umpires. Spectators stood by the sidelines and yelled until we were hoarse. Everybody carried a lemon. When you got hoarse, you sucked on the lemon.

My brother Stanley was part of a group of ten or twelve boys who were the sons of the leading businessmen in town. He was the most popular boy in the group. Each of the boys felt that Stanley was his best and closest friend.

Life was not easy for women in those days. All I can remember about my grandmother, my father's mother, was that she was old and sick. Or at least she seemed old to me at the time. She got sicker and sicker, and then she died.

My grandfather remarried after my grandmother died. He married Nettie Steinlein, my mother's aunt from St. Louis. She had visited in Henderson several times, and she was "down on her uppers," as they say. He asked my mother if she thought her aunt Nettie would come to Henderson to be his housekeeper. He was a well-to-do man with a large house and several servants, a maid, a cook, and a chauffeur. His housekeeper became his wife.

When she came to Henderson, Nettie couldn't even boil water. But Grandfather had a cook to do that sort of thing. All Nettie was supposed to do was to keep things running smoothly. Although Grandfather had a large house, it was what you might call an add-on house. I don't know how many rooms they started with, but when the family needed more space, they would simply add another room. You had to walk through the rooms to get to other rooms.

Even so, it was considered to be a showplace for the town and the time. He had special carpets made for the front rooms. The living room and dining room were long rooms with circular windows at the ends. They were similar to bay windows but were actually set into rounded walls. The carpets were long carpets with circular ends to match the size and the unusual shape of the rooms. There were real Tiffany chandeliers, beautiful French wicker furniture, and hand-carved wooden furniture. He even had a fish pond in the yard and at one time collected Japanese koi fish to stock it. He was a remarkable man. You ought to see the kind of books and records he kept! Everything was lined up so neatly and so properly.

My mother was an educated woman who had been a school-teacher in St. Louis. When she came to Henderson, she always had help to do the cooking and housework. There were no modern appliances, so ladies needed all the help they could get.

Our house was the first in Henderson to have indoor plumbing. We had a septic tank in the back yard. Everyone in town came to see it. At first, my father had all the woodwork painted white. When it got dirty, my mother had it painted black so it wouldn't show the dirt.

It was a two-story house, and the bathroom was upstairs. My paternal grandfather died about the time my sister Doris was born, and so my grandmother came to Henderson to live with us. She was really a one-of-a-kind beauty with lovely curly hair.

My father was always busy. If he wasn't working late at the store, he was playing bridge with other gentlemen. He had a great many civic responsibilities.

Mother was always busy. In those days, you raised children the hard way. You sterilized bottles, you sterilized the milk, you washed and boiled the diapers. Mother raised four children, so she didn't have much spare time. She did a lot of PTA work and always had the ladies' Saturday-night bridge games at our house. My sister Doris had a talent for playing bridge, and from the time she was twelve or thirteen years old, she was often asked to "fill in" when the ladies needed a fourth for bridge. Staying up to midnight to play bridge with the ladies was exciting for a girl whose usual bedtime was eight p.m.! Doris later enjoyed the avocation of being a bridge teacher and a Certified Duplicate Bridge Director. Our family traveled very little, and we never visited our relatives in St. Louis; they came to Texas to visit mother. Mother read and wrote a great many letters to her friends and family back in St. Louis. She could spell anything! My father wrote beautiful poetry but he never could spell.

Mother was always the one who took us places. She took us swimming and she taught us all to swim. There were some nice lakes near where we lived, and sometimes we would go swimming when we went to visit our relatives in Lufkin. Their name was Abrams. We would go to DiBoll on the other side of Lufkin, swim, and then come back to Lufkin at noon and eat with the relatives. That was a long trip!

There was a much larger Jewish congregation in Lufkin than we had in Henderson. My father's cousin had a ready-to-wear store. Her father was an Abrams and her mother was a Marwil, a sister to my grandfather.

Papa had a car. You had to snap the parts on to keep the rain from coming in. Papa would never admit it was raining until it was pouring down. Then, when he couldn't deny the rain any longer, he would get out and he would be so angry that he would grind his teeth. He would talk through his teeth while he was trying to snap those things on the car. He took after his father. My grandfather had a very high temper. When he got angry he would break dishes, and Papa was high-tempered, too.

We had never a congregation in Henderson. Mother was brought up in the Reform movement and had known Rabbi Stephen S. Wise when she was growing up. She had four books on the Torah that Rabbi Wise had written. When we were children, she would read to us from those four books during the High Holy Days. After I was grown, Mother and I would attend services together either in Kilgore or in Marshall.

When I was a child we didn't participate in the activities of the other congregations in the area. There's an old story that explains this. The Williams family, one of the Jewish families in Henderson, lost their little boy. Although the death of a young child was not as uncommon in those days as it is today, it was no less tragic. The grieving family took the little boy's body to Tyler for burial. The Jewish people of Tyler refused to bury the poor child unless payment for the burial was made in advance. I don't know what reason the Tyler people may have had to do such an unkind thing, but the Jewish people of Henderson were so incensed by this heartlessness that they went home and never returned.

Even though he was not involved with any formal Jewish religious organizations, Papa upheld the Jewish belief in "tsedakah," in the obligation to do charity and good deeds. My father and Mr. D. R. Harris, editor of the newspaper, were known to be the most charitable people in Henderson. If a beggar ever came to town, people would send him either to Mr. Harris or to my father.

In addition to being very literary and artistic, my father was an outstanding public speaker. My sister Doris told me that one of her fondest childhood memories was accompanying him on those Sunday nights when he had been invited to preach a sermon in a country church. Sister always sat proudly in the front pew and marveled at his knowledge of the Bible and how he knew exactly what to say to a group of farm people.

Papa was very civic-minded as well. He received a posthumous award from President John F. Kennedy. (It was posthumous in that it arrived shortly after the president had been assassinated.) He received the award for his work with the Polio Chapter. With his help, the Rusk County group had raised more money to fight polio than any other county in the United States.

Although he was not called to the army, my father found countless ways to serve his country during both the First and Second World Wars. He was secretary of the Rusk County Council of Public Safety. He was county chairman of the Liberty Bond drives in 1918, and chairman of the Victory Bond Drives in 1919. He was chairman of Red Cross campaigns and Salvation Army fundraising campaigns all during the 1920s. He was appointed to a committee that was charged with the task of supervising relief work when the Rusk County Public Relief Program was reorganized in 1931. He was appointed to the committee that organized the regulations for all the rationing in Rusk County during World War II. He also served on the parole board.

My father retired from the retail business in 1935 and was elected mayor of Henderson in 1936. He won the election because he knew so many people, he had helped so many people, was respected by so many people, and had done so much civic work. As mayor, he paved more streets than had ever been paved before. He was such a popular mayor that he served two terms.

He was mayor of Henderson when the New London School exploded on March 17, 1937. Nearly three hundred students and faculty members of the New London School were killed, and others were maimed and injured. They brought those poor people into town in open trucks with arms and legs missing. It was a terrible tragedy.

My father organized the relief fund and collected the money that was donated to assist the families and survivors. He also organized the New London School Memorial Association, which raised funds for the monument that was built in memory of the victims.

He was elected director of the First National Bank of Henderson in 1945. Three years later, he was elected chairman of the board, and he remained chairman of the board until 1965

I attended the University of Texas for one year but returned home and went to work in my father's store. My father had come home to work for his father, and so I came to work for my father.

I never had a room of my own when I was growing up. I was so tired of sleeping with my sister that the first thing I did when I went to work was to go out and buy myself my own bed. I bought a little narrow iron bed. The second thing I bought for myself was a black dress, because my mother always said that young girls shouldn't wear black. She said no one wears black except old people and those who are attending funerals.

I didn't meet many Jewish people until my daughter Francine was old enough to start the first grade in 1950. At that time there were two other Jewish families, the Gergers and the Rices, living in Henderson and they had children the same age as Francine. They were sending their children to religious school at Temple Beth Sholom in Kilgore, so I sent my daughter to religious school there also.

Even though the rest of the nation was suffering terribly, Henderson escaped the Great Depression of the 1930s because of the oil boom. The oil boom brought many changes to East Texas, and it also brought tremendous opportunities.

CHAPTER 21

Joe and Carrie Riff

Gathered from various sources:

Joe Riff and his partner, Mr. Packman, came to Longview in February 1931 to open a Palais Royal Ladies' Dress Shop.

He left his wife, Carrie Scher Riff, in Little Rock, Arkansas, and arrived in the rough oil boom town alone. He was fortunate enough to rent a room at one side of the courthouse square, within easy walking distance from the Palais Royal store, which was located one block down and diagonally across the square from his rented room.

Times were hard all over the country. As he walked to work each morning, he was obliged to step across the reclining bodies of less fortunate men and women who were sleeping out in the weather on the courthouse lawn, covering themselves as best they could with old newspapers and shreds of blankets.

The dress shop was so successful that he was soon able to send for his wife. He bought Packman out, enlarged the store, and eventually changed the name to "Riff's," carrying an expanded line of elegant, high-quality ladies' merchandise including furs and designer originals.

He brought his parents to Longview in approximately 1934, while the boom was well under way. They opened the Carolane Shop, another women's clothing shop.

Maintaining strong family ties, Joe and Carrie Riff encouraged his sister Leona Riff Denowitz and her husband Ben Denowitz to come to Longview, where they opened the shoe salon at Riff's. Ben Denowitz later expanded into his own shoe business, the Longview Shoe Store.

They also encouraged Carrie's brothers Abe and Nap Scher and their wives Thelma and Sally to come to Longview from Little Rock, Arkansas. Thelma worked in Joe's store. Nap Scher and a partner, Leon Gans, opened a haberdashery. Leon Gans bought Nap's interest in the haberdashery in 1940.

The Riffs' store grew to legendary stature, rivaling the Neiman-Marcus store of Dallas for high-quality merchandise and service.

CHAPTER 22

Jay Sosland

"I think many oilmen have something of the gambler's spirit to become involved in the business."

My parents were living in Kansas City when the depression hit. My father had been in the diamond business all his life, and he thought the oil boom would be a good place to start over, so he came to East Texas in 1930. Times were so bad he had to come here by riding the rails.

He heard that Tyler was the most acceptable town in the area, so he planned to settle there. It was pouring rain when he left the train and walked into a restaurant on the square in Tyler. He thought the sign on the wall said the special was a chicken sandwich. The food didn't look like chicken, but he was hungry and he knew he would have to spend his last coins to pay for it, so he ate it. He had finished eating when he realized it wasn't a chicken sandwich at all, it was a chitlin' sandwich! Although my dad didn't keep kosher, he didn't go out of his way to eat pork, either. He walked out of the restaurant, slipped on the wet street, and broke his leg. He said, "I paid for my sins. God struck me down in Tyler, Texas!" He got back on the train with his broken leg and came to Longview instead.

He went to the Rembert National Bank in Longview and talked Katie Todd into cashing a check for him. He said, "This check is not worth a darn, but as soon as you cash it, I'm going to buy a diamond with it. I'm going to sell that diamond and I'm going to come back and make the check good."

She let him have the money, and he never forgot that she had trusted him. While I was growing up, my whole family went to Ms. Todd's house at Christmastime every year to take her a lovely gift.

Dad rented a showcase in the Longview Drug Store. It was only a little space, but the oil wells were starting to come in, people had more money than they had ever seen, and they were in a hurry to spend it. Dad didn't even own a cash register. He was selling diamond jewelry so fast he just threw the money into the showcase. He would completely fill that showcase with cash! The rest of the world was suffering in the 1930s, but there was no depression in East Texas.

Dad was immediately successful, but I'm sure he got on the train and went home to visit my mother from time to time, because I was born in Kansas City in December 1931. My mother brought me to Longview on the train in a little white wicker basket when I was only six weeks old.

My father, Morris Sosland, and his brothers Sam and Abe originally came to America from Vilna, which was then part of Russia.

My mother, Etta Remer Sosland, was born in New York City. She grew up near Tremont Avenue in the Bronx, which was once a beautiful, elegant, elite suburban area. She was one of Hattie Carnagie's first hat designers.

I've heard many stories about my parents' courtship. People advised my mother not to marry my dad because he was "not her sort," but she loved him and she married him anyway. They were first married in a civil ceremony, but they always considered the anniversary of their religious wedding to be their formal wedding anniversary.

Dad and Herman Weinberg were partners. Herman was famous because he had the longest bar in Kansas City. When he found the business location in Longview, my dad called Herman and said, "Forget about Kansas City. This is the place to be. There's money everywhere!"

I don't know when their partnership was dissolved. Weinberg opened the Weinberg Men's Store in Kilgore, and Dad had the jewelry store in Longview. Herman's son, Joe Weinberg, later bought the Wiseman's Department Store in Marshall.

The first home I remember was on Sidney Street. We lived across the street from Dr. Ben Andres and the Dorfman family, who lived side by side in a duplex. The Dorfmans owned a St. Bernard dog that was so big I could ride it when I was three years old. One day I decided to go off on my own, riding on the dog. We went down to the creek to play and I was gone all day. My parents were terrified. Everyone in town was out looking for me, but they couldn't find me until the dog and I got ready to come home.

It wasn't difficult to be a Jewish kid in Longview during the oil boom. I never felt different or uncomfortable. In fact, I only had one bad experience. I was in high school before the days when anybody paid attention to the laws that separated Church and State, so sometimes the Church would intrude on our State education. One time, an evangelist came to speak at a school assembly. He started ranting and raving and carrying on in a way that I had never seen before. He said, "Anybody who doesn't believe in Jesus Christ, stand up."

I didn't believe in Jesus Christ, so I stood up.

I was the only Jew in the class, so he started to attack me. I was on the football team, and pretty soon the whole football team stood up beside me because I was one of them and he was an outsider who was attacking me. That's the only incident I remember, and it had nothing to do with the other kids. It had to do with an insensitive adult who wasn't even part of our school. The kids didn't have those problems. We got along well, and we are still friends.

There was one high school club that included representatives of the different religions. I was always a member of that club because I was the only Jew they could find. I wasn't the only Jewish student in the high school, though. Madeline Karchmer, who later became Madeline Covin, was Jewish. Charley Trigger worked for Sam Dorfman. He moved his family here in the early '30s and had two daughters in the high school, but it wasn't until the 1940s when they suddenly started attending services, that any of us found out they were Jewish.

My friends always looked forward to the opportunity to come to my house, both for friendship and for the food. My mother was a wonderful cook and a gracious hostess.

My mother and Elizabeth Dorfman were charter members of the local Charity League, which later became the Junior Service League, and finally the Junior League. They were social leaders, both in the Jewish community and in the community overall. Many ladies in

A festive Passover Seder at the home of Morris and Etta Sosland included all the members of their family. Standing, back row, left to right: Jay and and Dawn Sosland, Abe Sosland, Etta Sosland, Dusty Davis, Leonard and Helen Sosland. Helen is holding Deacon Davis. Seated: Steve, Marty, and Shallene Sosland, Abe Sosland, and Marcus Sosland.

—Photo courtesy of Dawn Sosland

town give my mother credit for bringing the social graces to the area. She knew how to set an elegant table and how to entertain graciously. That was how people here wanted to live, but they needed someone to show them how to do it

We had a thriving Jewish community here while I was growing up. At first, the men would teach religious education in the back rooms of their stores. After they built the Temple in Kilgore, we had some interesting rabbis.

Temple Beth Sholom in Kilgore was an extremely close-knit group of warm and caring people. The congregation included people from Kilgore, Longview, Gladewater, Henderson, and other smaller places, and it was more like a family than a religious congregation. There was a feeling of loving, of loyalty, of community. They had the best parties, dinners, and social occasions. When they needed to expand, Hyman Hurwitz found a honkeytonk which they "converted" into a social hall. They were a down-to-earth, hard-working congregation, nothing elite about them.

Temple Beth Shalom of Kilgore, Texas
—Courtesy of Mike and Gina Joseph

Marshall was an older, more established town. Temple Moses Montifiore was a Reform congregation, and the people there were a rather elite group with "Old South" attitudes, proud of who they were and what they had built. Rabbi Phillipsborn was the rabbi in Marshall. He officiated at my Bar Mitzvah in Kilgore in 1945.

The Marshall ladies had two big fundraisers. One was at Passover when their Sisterhood took orders for Passover supplies, which were not available in East Texas. The Kilgore group always ordered Passover supplies from the Marshall ladies. The other fundraiser was when the Jewish ladies of Marshall made Mexican enchiladas.

Some Jewish people in Longview attended services at the Marshall congregation, while others attended services at the Kilgore congregation. Some, like my father, supported both groups. Both the Kilgore and Marshall congregations eventually became part of Temple Emanu-El of Longview.

A number of Jewish oilmen were active in the East Texas field. At one time, the Sandler Oil Company owned as much oil property as anyone in this area. Harry Sandler and my father were close friends.

He was from Kansas City. He was in the oil production business here from the start. He owned a lot of production. He was an expansive man, and a huge gambler. I think many oilmen have something of the gambler's spirit to become involved in the business.

Henry Feldman was a big oilman, but he was also a big gambler. He was really smart in the oil business, but gambling was a sickness with him. He gambled his money, his business, everything. He earned and lost millions. He had two sons, Larry and Sam. Sam had multiple sclerosis. Larry grew up to become a stockbroker.

Sonnel Felsenthal started off north of El Dorado, Arkansas, and followed the oil boom towns until he got to Longview. His wife Annette's mother sang in the choir at the B'nai Zion Temple in Shreveport.

The Davis family from Tulsa, Oklahoma, owned Producer's Pipe and Supply Company, which was located near the railroad tracks. Sam Dorfman owned the Louisiana Pipe and Supply. He also co-founded Delta Drilling.

Sam Siegal's mother, Sam Dorfman, and the Sklar family were all related. Sam Siegel worked for Sam Dorfman. He knew the oil business inside and out. After World War II, in 1945, he went to Burma and discovered a tremendous oilfield there. Sam Weldman was in the oil business. Izzy Maritsky had a men's clothing store, but he was in the oil business in a big way.

The Schulman family was four brothers from Jackson, Tennessee, who all started out in the food business. They had a barbecue stand on Sixth Street. They later became wealthy when they discovered the oilfield at Cairo, Illinois.

Many of the Jewish oilmen were in the scrap iron business before they got into the oil business. Sam Dorfman was a major producer in the oilfield, but even he was in the scrap business before he became a producer. He came from Shreveport, and he brought a number of Jewish people here to work for him. He brought the Gardesbane family and Charley Trigger. Ben Balter worked for him.

People from all over the country came to Longview to buy diamonds from my father. He had accounts from coast to coast. During one of my wife Dawn's first trips here, we had to go out to the airport to deliver merchandise to the private plane of the Wise family of the Humble Oil Company. We had more accounts from Shreveport than any jewelry store in Shreveport. We had accounts in Dallas. In fact, when Stanley Marcus married his first wife, her wedding ring came from my dad's store! Neiman-Marcus didn't have a jewelry department then, and he wanted to buy the best-quality merchandise, so he bought the ring from my dad. There were so many Jewish merchants here that Longview and Kilgore were completely closed for the High Holy Days. It was amazing to see the whole town just close.

My uncle Abe Sosland had the Rich Right Cafe on Green Street, downtown near the railroad tracks, at the beginning of World War II. He baked really good bagels and Jewish breads. The army had just built Harmon Hospital. The Jewish people, like all the people in the community, were very patriotic. One of the streets at Harmon Hospital was named for my family. The Jewish people did everything they could to help the war effort and to make life easier for the boys in uniform, who were so far away from home. After doing all they could for all the boys, they turned around and did something special to help the Jewish boys.

Every Friday night, my uncle Abe served a Shabbos dinner for all the Jewish soldiers stationed at Harmon Hospital. He always made kreplach soup, stuffed cabbage, kugel, chicken. He really took care of them. It would not be right to talk about the Jews of East Texas if I didn't mention a "Righteous Gentile" who lived here in Longview. His good deeds received no public recognition, nor did he ever want public recognition. Shortly before World War II, Dr. Hurst rescued several Jewish refugees from certain death in Germany. He somehow managed to bring them to America with his own money, without help from any formal organization, and without fanfare, and gave them work in his clinic in Longview. One of them, Dr. Stern, was an Austrian Jew who lost everything when the Nazis came into power. Dr. Stern went to New York to become one of the foremost eye surgeons in America. I don't know how Dr. Hurst was able to help these people escape, but he knew it was the right thing to do, and somehow he did it.

CHAPTER 23

Nathan Waldman

"I was thrust into a boom town that looked like the Hollywood set for a Western movie, with wooden sidewalks, muddy streets, crowds day and night."

My parents, Joseph and Clara Waldman, came from an area of Austria near the Nyester River. When Franz Josef was emperor, he encouraged a normal style of living for all his people, so my parents did not leave Europe to escape religious persecution. They left because of love.

In those days, it was the custom for marriages to be arranged for young people by their families. My dad belonged to a family of prosperous farmers who were wealthy in the measure of land, livestock, and forests. My mother's father was the equivalent of a forest ranger—a different economic level. My dad's folks arranged a marriage for him, but he and my mother were already sweethearts.

Since she knew my father's family did not favor their marriage, my mother decided to go to the New World to seek her fortune. Although she had one sister living in America, she knew that she would be saying goodbye to her friends and family, to everything she knew and loved. It was a brave decision for a delicate young girl who was no bigger than a minute and who did not speak English.

My dad's family made all sorts of inducements to encourage him to stay, but he realized that if he was going to marry her, he had better follow her to America, because that was where she was going.

Mother came to New York to live with her sister. Dad came over on the same ship. They both traveled steerage. They had the kind of courage not many of us can even think about these days. Although he grew up as a pampered rich boy, when he arrived in New York City he had no money, no connections, and did not even know the language. Like other young people in those desperate circumstances, he did the only thing he could do. He went to work in the sweatshops.

A relative who knew my parents wanted to make a life together asked them both to come to Louisiana. They left New York, were married in Beaumont, Texas, and Dad immediately went to work in a general store in Gad, Louisiana, which was then an oil boom town. When she was expecting me, my mother went all the way to the hospital in Beaumont so that I would be born in Texas. Fortunately for me, it happened to be the nearest hospital.

I was only three years old when we left Louisiana, and my recollections of the place are vague. We lived in the back of the store. A mule kicked me. It was a fair fight. I hit him and he hit me back. Like any normal three-year-old, I waited until my mother was occupied and I wandered out into the street. I had a little ruler in my hand, so I gave the mule a smack. He returned the favor and gave me a smack. I learned an important lesson. You don't stand behind a mule if you are going to hit him with a ruler.

My parents learned to speak English rather quickly. Surprisingly, the people who once used to joke at my father's accent soon came to believe in him and to trust him. They came into the store to cash their paychecks and would leave their money with him for safekeeping.

My parents discovered it was impossible to maintain a normal religious life, which requires the presence of a viable Jewish community, so they moved from Gad to Beaumont, Texas. Dad worked hard and built his business until he had two stores in Beaumont, a shoe store and a big department store. But when the depression hit, it wiped him out overnight. One day there was a business, prosperity, success—and the next day there was nothing. After all their hard work they were right back where they started.

My dad took every kind of job trying to survive, but nothing worked. Then a relative offered to finance him if he would operate a

Joe Waldman pauses in his bookkeeping for a moment inside the crowded office of the Fair Store, Kilgore, Texas, February 1932.

—Photo courtesy of Florence Waldman

business in the boom town of Kilgore, Texas, a small agricultural community that had grown to fifteen thousand people within two weeks after the discovery of oil. In the face of a horrible global depression, Kilgore had customers who had the money to buy things. My dad and his relative found a gentleman who owned a general store, which had agricultural things like horse collars, washtubs, and plows. They had to buy him out so they could get his location. Other Jewish merchants came to Kilgore the same way. They had to buy an existing store for its location and then fill it with their own merchandise.

Gladewater, Longview, and Henderson were all booming, but Kilgore was the center of oil activity, the actual drilling, and the pipe and supply houses. Most of the time, men came to the area alone. When they established a business and found a place to live, they sent for their families.

Since our store was across the street from the depot, we could watch the trains from our door as they came into town. Every train would bring scores of men riding the rails, come into town looking for work. If there were any women, you didn't see them because they didn't come to town. You mostly saw men on the streets. There were women who lived in the community before the boom. There were wives of the businessmen who came with the boom, but it wasn't until a few years after the boom had settled down that the women came into their own as organizers to establish clubs and social organizations.

My dad arrived in Kilgore in 1930, during my senior year in high school in Beaumont, and as soon as I graduated, Mother and I followed him. I attended high school in what you might consider a "normal" environment, but I was suddenly thrust into a boom town that looked like the Hollywood set for a Western movie, with wooden sidewalks, muddy streets, crowds day and night. The stores were all open until midnight.

My mother never questioned living in such a wild place. She taught herself to type on an upright Royal typewriter. She taught herself to keep books. She was always interested in civic affairs, although she worked so hard that she didn't have time to participate in as many activities as she would have liked.

Everybody in town turned out for the big celebration when the first downtown Kilgore block was paved. That was the only street that was paved. The roads were mostly mud because of the frequent rains, and, since cars and trucks couldn't get through the mud, mule-drawn and horse-drawn wagons were used. Two days after the big celebration, the mud covered that one little piece of paving so that you would never know it was there.

A shantytown was set up in what is now a city park. There were lines for everything. There was one bath house, and there were long lines to get into it. There was one public bathroom. They charged to use it, and there was a long line for that, too. There were long lines in front of every cafe because there were so few eating places and so many hungry people.

Oil well drilling was allowed within the city limits. Downtown Kilgore and the area immediately around it had 1,200 producing wells. If you were drilling a successful well and I owned the lot next to you, you were taking oil from my deposit. So by law, I could put down what is called an "offset well." The guy over on this side of me was also entitled to "offset" my well. Oil wells were thick as picket fences because there were all these little plots of land owned by different people. When regulation stepped in, such things were no longer possible.

I remember when they cut the ends off the buildings that covered half a city block in downtown Kilgore and leveled the block so that wells could be put up behind the buildings. That was called "the World's Richest Half Acre." For years, passing trains would slow down just to point it out.

They drilled a well right outside our windows. Drilling was on a twenty-four-hour time schedule. When they started drilling, they never stopped. Oh, how the building shook! They were going down into the earth with tremendous force. That kind of drilling was going on constantly on that half-block. I wouldn't believe it was possible, but eventually, you learned to fall asleep with the sound.

With all of that, it wasn't frightening. There was no fear in the sense that we know it today, when people lock themselves up inside their homes and are afraid to walk on the streets. People weren't afraid because we had a common denominator. Everybody was poor. Everybody had the same problems: food, water, housing, jobs.

There was a great deal of rowdiness, gambling, and crime, but those who shot other people didn't walk around with guns on their hips. The rowdiness exploded at the honkytonks and places like that, not out on the streets.

One time, my dad prevented a man from killing someone. He simply talked him out of it. The men were good friends, and the man was so relieved that he hadn't killed his friend that he gave Dad his pistol. It was never fired.

There was a bit of theft, though. Since the oilfield workers didn't believe in banks, the Jewish merchants became their bankers because they knew the merchants were honest people they could trust. On payday, the merchants would cash their checks. This meant it was necessary to keep a lot of cash on hand on payday, and the crooks all knew when payday came around.

Although robberies were rare, my folks were once robbed at gunpoint. It was a frightening experience. Stairs led up to our apartment above the store, and at the base of the stairs there was a little office and the safe. The robbers came into the store and marched my parents to the stairs at the back and had them sit down. My mother had her diamond ring exposed, and Dad kept trying to call her attention to it, trying to warn her to turn the ring around. It became so obvious that the robber finally said, "Don't worry, mister. We would never take a lady's ring. All we want is your money."

There was a desperate need for law and order, so the Texas Rangers came into town. The Texas Rangers have a well-known saying, "One riot, one Ranger." Well, Kilgore got so bad we had to have fifteen Rangers all at one time. There was no jail, so they chained prisoners to a pole outside one of the churches.

There lots of stories about the Lone Wolf, Texas Ranger "Lone Wolf" Gonzaullas, but the scene that stands out in my mind is a prime example of the man's incredible bravery. Our store had a narrow stairway going up to the second floor. A gunman pulled a robbery in town and ran up those stairs to take refuge. Lone Wolf walked directly up those stairs all by himself, without any backup, and he came down with that gunman. I always wondered what power kept him from getting shot. I guess the gunman was simply afraid to shoot him.

The Rio Palm Isle is an offshoot of what used to be called "Mattie's Ballroom," which was the best place to go dancing, and Mattie Castleberry handled it with an iron rule. All the big bands played at Mattie's Ballroom in the thirties and forties, and people came there from all over East Texas and western Louisiana during the boom and during the good times that followed.

There were some nice homes in Kilgore before the oil boom, in the Victorian style of architecture with porches and columns. At first, my family lived in a room over a store in a little two-story building in which the lower levels were businesses and the upper levels were rooms. From there, we moved into a "shotgun" house. These were small frame houses, but they were quite an improvement over living in one little room. Eventually, we moved into larger quarters when the post office, which was located next door to the store, moved and we took it over. It was twice the size of the original store, and we moved into the little apartment above it.

I think our first real home was brick, and it was built at a cost of $1,100. With two bedrooms, a living room, dining room, kitchen, and one bath, it was a nice house, much like anybody else's house in those days.

There were Jewish people living in East Texas before the boom, but none of them lived in Kilgore. As the oil boom progressed, the

Jewish community grew, but there was no organized religious service. When someone would have a Jartzeidt (the annual anniversary of a loved one's death during which special prayers are traditionally offered), he would want to say prayers in memory of the deceased. Ten men would be called together to form a Minyan so they could pray. We would meet at Sam Goldman's store, which was also where the Sunday school met, or at Ben Gertz's toggery store, or at Eddie Ettelman's Jewelry store, or at Hymie Hurwitz's men's shop. It may seem strange that we held the Minyans at the stores, but we did so because we had noplace else to go. Minyans were normally held at six o'-clock when the men were ready to go home to eat supper. They would leave their stores, go to the Minyan, and then go home to supper.

Of course, the stores could not be closed at suppertime. Someone had to stay at the store, so families couldn't even eat together. It was a hard life, but when you're that busy, you don't have time to notice how hard life is. East Texas was the economic focal point of the whole country. I can't even begin to convey the excitement of being there, then.

Our first High Holiday services were held above the fire station downtown. We never had a quiet service, because every time the fire trucks turned on their sirens, the people would run to the windows to see where the fire might be and if they needed to help.

We had some scholarly people in Kilgore who were the intellectual equivalent of Ben Balter in Longview. Ben Gertz was a highly educated man who was fluent in Hebrew, and he or his brother Abe would conduct services. Our services were simple and straightforward, but we were simple people, and we all went home feeling much the better for having been part of them. It was interesting to note that once the earliest part of the boom was over and life began to settle down, the High Holy Days closed the town. All the Jewish merchants closed their businesses for the High Holy Days, so you'd just as well not bother to go downtown in Kilgore or Longview or any other East Texas town to shop.

Although there were eventually some people who did not choose to close their businesses in respect for the High Holy Days, such people were few and far between. We did not respect them, and our neighbors in the Christian community quickly lost their respect for them, as well.

The community began to organize about the time I went away to college. The Jewish ladies formed an organization before the Temple was built and were very active in the creation of the Temple. Mrs. Anne Rose was greatly responsible for the fact that they built a Temple at all. Her husband, Bernard Rose, was in the scrap metal business, and one day she called all the women together at her house behind the scrap yard to discuss setting up a formal religious school for the children.

The ladies raised some of the money, and the men matched what the ladies had raised. They borrowed money, bought property, and Congregation Beth Sholom opened the doors of its new building in 1936. We were the only Jewish organization in the Kilgore, Longview, Gladewater, Overton, Henderson area. Later, Hymie Hurwitz found a wood frame honky-tonk, which was bought and moved next to the Temple to be our social hall.

They imported a very young Orthodox rabbi. Of course he wouldn't ride on the Sabbath. He wouldn't carry as much as a hand-kerchief. He wouldn't even walk under a telephone line, although I never heard of anybody else with that particular prohibition. This didn't pose too much of a problem in Kilgore, since we didn't have that many phones in town, so he could easily walk where he wanted to go without walking under any telephone lines.

In those days there was a fenced pasture behind the Temple on what is now the campus of Kilgore College. It was a pleasant, well-kept pasture, and the Temple's Christian neighbor kept a nice-looking horse there. That young rabbi was dreadfully afraid of that horse, and I'm afraid the horse was not too crazy about him, either. The synagogue was at one end of the fenced pasture, and the rabbi lived directly at the opposite end. One day when he was late for serv-ices, the rabbi decided to take a shortcut through the pasture from his house to the synagogue. That horse took umbrage at the invasion of his personal domain. The horse started running toward the rabbi, and the rabbi started running toward the synagogue. The horse ran faster and the rabbi ran faster, and before you knew it, he managed to prove that when properly motivated, an Orthodox rabbi can run faster than a Christian horse.

The Jewish young people I knew were away at school at the University of Texas. Joe Hirsch from Marshall had sisters who were my age, and I met them at the university. There were only a few of us. Those who were Jewish and roughly my age worked so hard that we had precious little time for social activity. What did I do as a young college person, other than work? I worked some more. In the summertime I would come home from college to work in our store, and I would spend my Christmas "vacations" working in our store. The stores were open from early morning until twelve o'clock at night, so there wasn't much of what you'd call "leisure time" to worry about.

One time, when I was home for "vacation," I was offered fifty dollars to baby-sit a well. Fifty dollars for a night's work was big money. Those were the days of "hot oil." They were running oil when they shouldn't, and they had to have somebody there to turn that valve off quickly in case the patrols came by. Unfortunately, my parents heard about it and I wasn't able to take the job.

Our business was called the Fair Store. It was the forerunner of today's department stores in that we catered to all members of the family and all levels of society. We had tablecloths which sold for as much as one hundred fifty dollars—an unheard-of luxury at a time when a pair of good khaki pants cost only ninety-nine cents.

Our customers were both what you would call the "nicer" people in town and the harder-working oilfield people. By the very nature of his work, a roughneck is going to be a little unkempt. He may not shave as often as he should, and his work is hard and dirty. Oilfield workers are often oily.

The drugstore across the street had a long bar with a foot rail alongside of it, just like you'd see in the Western movies. You'd see some of these big, rough, tough, unshaven oilfield men go in, put a foot up on the bar rail, and order a malted milk. I thought that was hilarious!

For the most part, those who suddenly became millionaires were just regular people. They may have enhanced their way of living, but they were just people.

Early on, there were shortages of everything. It was hard to get merchandise because of problems with transportation; since the stores were small and your audience was overwhelming, the stores frequently ran out of merchandise. Dallas was the source of supply. I remember my folks riding to Dallas by train to buy merchandise and coming back the same day. They ordered merchandise and had it delivered. If it was something special, they carried it with them on the train. You had to go to Gladewater to take the train to Dallas, although I could take the train from Kilgore to go to school in Austin. The roads were not good, so trains were a good way to travel.

The Jewish merchants who went into the oil business were the more enterprising people, the people who had money and the people who were gamblers at heart, people like Hymie and Sam Hurwitz, or Bill and Harry Golden. Most didn't actually drill the wells—they invested in oil ventures. The truly big Jewish oilmen like Mayor Bodenheim and Izzie Maritsky, those who really hit it big, were over in Longview. The others were buying a piece of royalty here and there. If you had the money and you had the contacts, and if you were willing to take a gamble, oil was the thing to do. Unfortunately, my folks were not gamblers. They had other places to put what little money they had, such as my education.

We don't talk to our parents when we have them. There are so many things we could have asked our parents and we didn't. As a teenager, you just don't realize how your parents are sacrificing their needs for yours. I didn't appreciate the hard work my parents did to get me through school. It's only too late that you realize what they went through to send you to school, what they had to sacrifice to keep you in school. It's a wonderful thing to think about.

When we were living in the little shotgun house, there was a disastrous fire that almost leveled the block containing our store, a barbershop, and the buildings all the way to the corner. The firemen actually stopped the fire in the barbershop.

We heard the noise and saw the flames. Nobody had a telephone, but somebody came running and told us our store was on fire, and we ran to see if we could take some things out. The firemen would not let us go into the building. I went around the back and sneaked in, and of all the things, I brought out a camera. I took pictures. You can't recognize anything you're looking at, but I got a picture of that fire.

There was another time in the wild days when an arsonist was loose in town. He burned down three churches on one terrible Sunday. The firemen would go to fight one fire, and then somebody would report that another church was on fire. The story that circulated was that the authorities found the arsonist and spirited him out of town because they were afraid the crowds would lynch him. And they probably would have done it, too. Tempers were high.

There were major oil well fires, but I think it was something of a miracle that none of them was right in town. With all those wells right in the middle of town, there could have been a terrible disaster. I did see one horrible oilfield disaster. I went to an outdoor arena one evening to attend a wrestling match. My seat faced the arena, and you could look way out into the field beyond it. A well exploded out there in the field. It caught fire and it blew, just like that. In plain sight, just as though you'd put it on display and arranged it.

Everybody at the wrestling match ran to try to do what we could do to help fight the fire. One workman had been blown off the platform. He wasn't actually on fire, but he was so close to the flames that they were burning him to death, and the firemen couldn't reach him. They had all kinds of shields, they had all kinds of water, but they couldn't reach him in time to save him. The poor man burned to death before our eyes.

Sisters Adele Rutstein and Sarah Rutstein Pfeffer are seen against the background of an oilfield fire in Kilgore, Texas.

—Courtesy of Mike and Gina Joseph

The streets were always crowded. You could see the cosmopolitan influence as more and more people drifted into town. Once the boom settled in, people had free time to further cultural pursuits, and they established a library, the Community Concert Series, various women's organizations that did good works. There was a movie house in the block that burned up. Later, there were others. I didn't have time to go to the movies because my whole family worked so hard.

When the Crim Theater opened, all the Hollywood stars were in attendance because, as a member of one of those old families in the community who got rich in oil, Mr. Crim made sure all the famous big-time Hollywood stars came here for opening night. There were searchlights flooding the skies, ladies in ball gowns, men in tuxedos . . . It was something amazing for Kilgore, Texas.

Mr. Crim also was a powerful mainstay of the Community Concert Series because he would pay the money to make up the deficit. He did the same thing later when they founded the famous Kilgore College Rangerettes drill team, sponsoring them on many of their trips to distant places.

Kilgore's Community Concert Series was remarkable— some really big names, beautifully talented artists, famous headliners in the nation, internationally famous performers. They all came to play concerts in the high school auditorium in Kilgore, Texas. This was during the depression, and they knew that in Kilgore, unlike many other places, they would get paid.

The Jewish people were always active participants in the community's cultural affairs, backing the things that were good. Frances Gertz, for example, took important leadership roles in many cultural activities. For a long time she was the spearhead of the Community Concerts and was called "Mrs. Community Concert." She was a dynamic woman, and nobody could deny her anything she asked for.

Jewish families were active and interested in the growth of the city. Harry Golden, Henry Feldman, Hymie Hurwitz, Ben Gertz, Sol Finkelstein, Eddie Ettelman, Sam Golden, and all their wives are only a few of the names which come to mind as leaders of the Jewish community.

Sam Goldman was a gruff, rough, big man—big in the sense of bulky, not tall. He was big-hearted as well. And jovial, but you played dice with him at your own risk. There was something about that game for him, or the opportunity to win.

People in this town were too busy to be anti-Semitic. There was no ugliness. For the most part, most of these people had never met a Jew before the oil boom. In small, rural communities, people probably pick up their anti-Semitism from what they have been told by their preachers who were interpreting the Bible incorrectly. Here in Kilgore, we have always had ethical, well-educated clergymen, which might account for the absence of anti-Semitism here

There was only one ugly incident that I can remember. During World War II, when the editor of the daily paper went away to the army, his wife temporarily took over. Some terribly offensive things came out in print. Hymie Hurwitz went to the newspaper and objected to a particular headline she had printed. But he was not alone, since most of the Christian people in town were offended by it as well, and they let her know they would not put up with that sort of nastiness. Her personal anti-Semitism did not reflect this community or the people here. Basically that was one woman's problem and she had to deal with it. The people in Kilgore didn't think of the Jewish people as anything other than friends and neighbors, part of the community and part of their lives.

Much of this was because we participated in the community. Doing your part is important. I was on the board of the Chamber of Commerce; Hymie Hurwitz, often called "Mr. Kilgore," was president of the Chamber; Hyman Laufer was active in the Lions Club. In Longview, Dave Bergman was active on the hospital board, the Boy Scouts, and everything else good in the community. Ralph Cohen was president of the Cancer Society. The list goes on and on and on.

I believe this attitude accounted for what I can only call "the Great Kilgore Shoe Day." It happened during World War II while I was away in the army. At that time, sugar, gasoline, and everything else you needed to survive was rationed. One Sunday morning, the announcement came over the radio that the following day they would start rationing shoes. When you woke up on Monday morning, you would no longer be able to buy a pair of shoes without having the proper number of very limited ration coupons.

The phone rang at our house. One of my dad's customers, a friend and neighbor, called Dad with an emergency request. He was going out of town on an unexpected trip, and he had to have a new pair of shoes to take with him. Although the stores were closed on

Sundays due to the Blue Laws, Dad was always willing to help a customer or a friend with a problem. He said, "Meet me at the store. I'll open up for you and I'll fix you up with some shoes."

No sooner had he sold that man a pair of shoes than he saw six more good friends and customers waiting at the door. And then there were a dozen more, and twice that, and even more. It was like a small crack in a dam that a drop of water seeps through and before you turn around, you're caught up in a raging flood that overwhelms you.

By noon, every store in town was open for business, all of them selling shoes, just shoes, nothing but shoes. People came with their wives and their children, and they bought as many pairs of shoes as they could possibly buy. They bought every style, and every color and size, and they bought the next two or three sizes for the children to grow into. By evening, there was not a pair of shoes to be had, in any size or any style, anywhere in Kilgore, Texas. Nobody had ever seen a shoe day quite like that one.

The oil derricks that lined the streets of downtown Kilgore were always decorated with beautiful Christmas lights. At one particular place at the depot they would string the words "Happy New Year" in lights between the derricks. They would leave the lights up all year long so they wouldn't have to restring them, although they did not turn them on until the holiday season arrived in December.

As it happened, they were testing those lights when Rabbi Dan Kerman arrived in the fall, shortly before the High Holy Days. We were driving around town to show our new rabbi what Kilgore looked like. We drove by this huge, brilliantly lighted sign saying, "Happy New Year." The rabbi couldn't get over the fact that the people of Kilgore would do such a nice thing for the Jewish community on the High Holy Days. Since they would have done it if they had thought about it, we saw no reason to tell him otherwise.

CHAPTER 24

Sarah Richkie Whitehurst

"I still had my bedroom when I came home, but lots of my friends didn't. Everybody rented rooms to the strangers who came in with the boom."

I was away at college when "Dad" Joiner's oil well came in at Joinerville near Turnertown in Rusk County. By the time I came home at Christmas, everything was bursting at the seams—literally! It rained day and night, so the wooden blocks that paved Longview's downtown streets were popping up with the rain and the streets were going every which way.

At least when I came home, I still had my bedroom, but lots of my friends didn't! So many strangers came in with the boom, and everybody rented rooms to them, so there might be four or five strange men living in a house, two or three of them to a room. Because housing was so tight, not only did people rent out rooms, but some people rented spaces in their bedrooms or parlors. There would be strange people sleeping on the dining room floors! Others rented beds in shifts. A man could sleep in the bed so many hours, and then he'd have to get up so somebody else could sleep. Some people were charging two hundred dollars a week—in those days— for a small room. My mom and dad couldn't overcharge people like that. They never charged more than they thought a bed or a house or anything else was worth. I guess it was because Dad came up the hard way.

My father, Louis Richkie, was a tailor, born in Austria, near Vienna, December 25, 1880. My mother, Nellie Henry Heidtman, was born in Taylorsville, Kentucky, on September 26, 1875. They met in Sulphur Springs, Texas, in 1903. Here's how my father from Austria and my mother from Kentucky wound up meeting in Sulphur Springs.

Mama's first husband died three months before her second child was born, so she had to go back to Sulphur Springs to live with her parents. My grandma taught school, so Mama took care of the house, and she earned money by making buttonholes. You see, there was no such thing as a zipper in those days. Every Monday, Mama would walk down to Mr. Richards' tailor shop on the square in Sulphur Springs, where she would pick up coats, vests, and trousers to mend. She would take the clothing home and work the buttonholes. The next Monday she would go to the tailor shop to be paid for her finished work and pick up more work to do.

My dad was an itinerant tailor who went from one place to another. He landed penniless and almost unclaimed in the United States—but he wasn't completely unclaimed, because he had an aunt in New York City. He realized he would not be able to develop himself in the sort of environment New York City offered at that time, so he only stayed until he earned enough money to leave. At one time he was in Houston, but the climate was bad for him. He may have gone to Sulphur Springs from Houston.

Although he was very good at his trade, he hadn't gone beyond a third-grade formal education. He could make numbers and he could write his name, but he didn't get far enough in school to learn to write properly. He couldn't spell, but he could read anything you put before him. He could work percentages and math problems in his head. When he measured a customer, he could write the measurements perfectly.

Then one day in the tailor's shop in Sulphur Springs, my father, who cut patterns and materials, met my mother, who worked buttonholes by hand! They realized that they were a perfect match, and they were married on April 2, 1905. They lived and worked together fifty-six years, two weeks, and two days.

Between them, their children were two sons and three daughters:

Frank Henry Heidtman, Col. Ralph Malcolm Heidtman, Mary Richkie Finlay, Sarah Richkie Whitehurst, and Rosa Richkie Lamb. Dad was always eager for the family to be together because he believed, as he would tell us, "An earthly family is but a small representation of the larger family of God." I sometimes wonder, if my father had a son of his own, would he have wanted to bring him up in the Jewish faith? But we will never know, because he had three little girls. Although he always remained a faithful Jew, he believed strongly in religion and he encouraged us to go to church with our mother. I was raised in the First Christian Church.

My parents lived in Corsicana for sixteen months before they came to Longview in the summer of 1906. While they were in Corsicana, Papa saw an ad in the *Dallas News* stating that a Mr. Sternberg, a tailor in Longview, Texas, wanted to hire a cutter and coatmaker. Papa came to Longview, applied for the job, and Mr. Sternberg hired him. Mama was expecting my sister Mary, so she and her two little boys returned to her parents' home in Sulphur Springs to birth her third baby, her first with Dad. After the recuperation, Mama came to Longview.

Mr. Sternberg had a little business in a wood frame building that fronted on Bank Alley. During that year, Mr. Sternberg developed what they then called "consumption," which was actually tuberculosis, so he had to leave this damp East Texas climate. He approached Dad about buying the business. I don't know how they possibly could have done it, but my parents had managed to save the lordly sum of two hundred dollars. Unfortunately, Mr. Sternberg was asking five hundred dollars. They had nothing more to offer him, but it was buy the business or lose Papa's job.

Although they were desperate, Mama was always able to keep Dad's morale up, and this instance was no exception. Mama attended the Christian Church with the C. C. Morgan family. One of their four sons was president of the First National Bank. She told Dad she felt certain that he could go to Mr. Crawford Morgan and tell him about his ambitions and desires, and Mr. Morgan would help him.

Since Dad and Mama were both unbelievably modest, never calling attention to themselves, asking for help from someone was a terribly hard thing for them to do, but it had to be done. When Dad got up his courage and went to see Mr. Morgan, Mr. Morgan put his arm on my father's shoulder, and said, "Son, you haven't got any prob-

lems. I think we can take care of it." With that, he took him into the
bank and convinced his son, the bank president, to let Mom and Dad
have five hundred dollars with no security except that Mr. Morgan
signed the loan for them. Mom and Dad never forgot that. They
worked tirelessly until they repaid that loan. The families remained
friends from that time on.

So my papa started business on his own in the little building on
Bank Street, later moving into the building above the K. Wolens
store. He had the entire second floor of the brick building on the
east side of Fredonia Street south of the T&P Railroad tracks. The
firm grew to employ thirty professional tailors making coats, vests,
trousers, and overcoats. They were the only custom tailors in
Longview. In 1922, Dad moved his business across the railroad tracks
and downstairs to a brick building in midblock. There was a barbershop next to it, and on the corner was the Duke and Ayers nickel
store, where you could find everything you needed for a nickel. The
salespeople behind the counters would help you.

This was a farming area, and cotton was ginned right here in
Longview, at the cottonseed mill across the tracks on Cotton Street.
In addition to the cotton, three railroad lines came into Longview.
Longview's economy depended heavily on the railroad division. We
had the big roundhouse. The brakemen and conductors all wore blue
serge suits. At that time a blue serge suit was a necessity in every gentleman's wardrobe. Almost every man bought two pairs of trousers
with a vest and coat, which made a four-piece suit. My dad would
buy blue serge by the five-hundred-yard bolt. He had to shrink it
himself, because fabrics were not pre-shrunk in those days. Mama
still did all the buttonholes.

With five children, my parents had to be careful. They were not
"stingy," but they were frugal, sound, and sensible. They disciplined
themselves. Even after we all married, every time we talked about
buying something, Mom and Dad would ask, "Can you pay for it?"
You would save until you had the money to buy what you needed. If
you didn't have the money, you couldn't buy it, no matter how much
you wanted or needed it. I sometimes think it would be a tremendous
adjustment to them to see how things are now. This national indebt-
edness would be a shock. I never heard my mother say, "I want this
new hat or this dress and I'm going to have it. You children are going
to have what you need, but I'm going to have this for myself."

She was a beautiful woman, but she worked hard, hard, hard. She had beautiful skin, and she did nothing to her face but wash it with soap and water. The Christmas before she died, my brother's child gave Mama a bottle of Hind's honey and almond cream. She would just look at that in amazement. It was the first face cream she ever owned. It was a luxurious gift to her.

My dad was handsome. He was five foot eight or nine and sturdy. He had black curly hair and dark eyes. He had a deep, gruff voice, but if you ever looked at his eyes you'd know he wasn't angry. As long as Dad lived, his great indulgence would be four cigars a day. They were were El Producto Excepcionales, and they cost twenty-five cents apiece. When these particular cigars became scarce, Doc Russo, the pharmacist, would get them for Dad.

At first, they lived in a small frame rent house on East Cotton Street. I couldn't tell you the extent of their finances, because my parents didn't talk about this kind of thing and would never do any bragging, but by hard work and careful planning, Mom and Dad were eventually able to buy their own home on East South Street, where they lived for forty-three years. They were able to buy some real estate, as well—and rent houses of one kind or another. They were never speculative people, and they did not ever invest in farmland. Dad was not a farmer, and he didn't know anything about farming.

When the oil boom came, Mom and Dad had saved some money, and they indulged in nothing but proven royalties. They weren't greedy, and they believed in not wanting to have more than anybody else, and they didn't believe in gambling their hard-earned money away. Some people were involved in chance-taking deals, but they were not. As it happened, some of what they bought was in the core of the first production. My dad and Mama talked things over and didn't fight or fuss or fall out. They never regretted what they did or didn't do.

The Lathrop A-1 well in the Pine Tree area was the third discovery well in the field. The oil was there, but it was just was not coming in. In those days, oil wells were not controlled as they are now. When they came in, we said they "blew," which means they gushed out wildly. They were wooden derricks, and sometimes the derricks caught fire. This well was still drilling, still hopeful, but it did not blow in.

As my dad fitted different promoters for their suits in his shop, they would talk about their work and their rigs. A lot of people who invested in that Lathrop well thought they were losing their money and tried to sell their interests to Dad, in fact, no less than an hour before that well blew in. But Mama and Dad said they didn't know anything about farms and they had never bought farmland before, so they didn't buy it.

They never regretted that they hadn't bought it, or how much more money they could have had if they had bought it. It was a good lesson for me to learn. I'm slow to make up my mind, but once I make it up I tell myself, You were deliberate in this and you thought it was the thing to do, so you shouldn't have regrets. What good does it do to regret something you haven't done? You won't get the chance to go back and rectify it.

Although Marshall was larger than Longview, there was some communitywide competition between the two towns, but it was friendly competition. Marshall has been able to capitalize on its historic significance. Tyler, on the other had, was smug back then. The people there still are. They just can't help it. I think it must be in their water.

Tyler was not in the original oil production area. It was a long time before there was any oil discovered near there, and never to the same extent as here, but they had civic-minded people who went after the oil company offices and brought them to Tyler. So it turned out that the working people lived closer to the oilfield, in Longview, Kilgore, Henderson, and Gladewater, and the "big shots" lived in Tyler.

My parents were not people who wanted to be showy. Mama and Dad were either at home, or at the shop, or involved with their church and synagogue connections. There was never an argument about religion in our household. They respected each other's religion. When I was older, Dad and I would talk about philosophy and religion. My father would ride the train to attend religious services at Temple Moses Montifiore in Marshall. He wasn't able to go every Friday night, but he was always able to go for the High Holy Day services.

At some point, before we had the Temple here in Longview, High Holy Days services were held in the room above the Knights of Pythias Hall. When they had services there, Mother used to go with Dad and I would go along with them.

After the oil boom, the number of Jewish families increased in the area. People from Longview, Kilgore, Overton, Arp, Troup, and other towns got together and built the Temple in Kilgore. Later, they built the Temple in Longview.

There were only a few Jewish families in Longview when I was growing up. There was a family named Levinson in the scrap business. There was a family named Friedlander. Max and Henry Friedlander were brothers who had bakery shops in town, and they baked delicious things. Then there was Mr. Edwin Bodenheim, who proclaimed loud and long until the day he died that he was a Jew, but I don't know that I ever met him in a Jewish worship service. He went to the Methodist Church with his wife, and he had a lot to say about, "Here I am, a Jew attending the Methodist Church with a Catholic daughter-in-law."

Mr. Bodenheim was the exact opposite of Dad. Dad was modest and humble, Mr. Bodenheim was loud and showy. Dad made Mr. Bodenheim's clothes. He was a flashy dresser, very colorful. He wore a red carnation in his lapel all the time.

Mr. Bodenheim had a wonderful salesman's personality, and he went into the insurance business. He built his home in the most dramatic spot in town, right at the point of Fredonia and Main. His wife was a local girl and a lovely lady. The suffered a lot, though, losing several children, who are buried at the Greenwood Cemetery with a little angel on the gravestones. They raised two sons, Edwin and Roland. Edwin's wife, Betty, came from Wichita Falls. They met while he was at Shepherd Air Force Base. Roland married a local girl, Josephine Hopkins, whose father was in the mercantile business in Longview.

Although they had very different personalities, my dad and Mr. Bodenheim were always good friends with a real admiration for each other. Each type of person makes contributions to life.

One time, Dad got his feelings hurt. He went to the First National Bank every day to make a deposit. You didn't normally have to make out deposit slips. The teller would take your money and record the deposit for you. He was standing there at the teller's cage when the teller thrust a deposit slip at him and demanded that he fill it out. Of course, that embarrassed Dad because he couldn't do it. He left and never went back. Mama took up making daily bank deposits after that.

In their own quiet way, my parents helped many people in this area, mostly people in the railroad business. The brakemen and switchmen would have seniority built up, and sometimes the motorman would get what you would call "bumped." This meant he didn't work. You didn't get paid when you didn't work, and you didn't strike in those days. Your family had to do without.

Mom and Dad loaned many of these people money. When people couldn't make their payments, Mom and Dad never foreclosed on them. They just told them, "You do the best you can and pay me when you have the money." And of course, they always did.

My parents did a lot of good for others, but they never wanted to call attention to themselves and were terribly embarrassed when others did so. So far as I know, I've never heard one unkind or disrespectful thing said about my mother or my father.

Mama died April 16, 1961, and my father died on May 4, 1964, at the age of eighty-four. His memorial service was given by the rabbi and two Protestant ministers. Newspaper publisher Carl Estes wrote an editorial titled, "Louis Richkie," in the *Longview Daily News*, May 7, 1964. In it, he described my dad as "exemplifying the truism that where there's a will, there's a way. Coming to America from his native Austria while he was a young man of twenty years of age, he was guided by destiny to Longview, a small town with few opportunities to offer a stranger from a foreign land. He was a man of ambition and desire. These attributes spurred him onward as he worked tirelessly in the tailor shop he opened to achieve the goal of which he had dreamed before coming to this country. Louis Richkie was a quiet, modest, unassuming man who had aspirations of becoming a useful citizen and a successful businessman even before reaching maturity. It was this desire that brought him to Longview in 1906 and the same inspiration that kept him active in his advanced years."

Index

A

A. Harris, 137
A. M. Byers Company, 30
Adams, Dr., 63
Ahavath Achim Synagogue, 115
Ammerman, Herschel, 99
Ammerman, Penni, 99
Ammerman, Rebecca, 99
Ammerman, Sarah, 99
Ammerman, Usha, 99
Andres, Anna Slayfield, 18
Andres, Bea, 13, 14, 18, 101
Andres, Ben, 7, 13-18, 90, 137, 174
Andres, David, 14, 101, 158
Andres, Isaac, 18
Andres, Joyce, 14
anti-Semitism, 106, 191
Antwell, Ann, 57
Antwell, Ben, 38, 57
Antwell, Charles, 57
Antwell, Jerrell, 57
Arnold, Arthur, 57

B

Back, Sophie, 104
Back, William, Sr., 104
Bailey, Molly, 145
Balter, Ace, 28, 34, 37, 44, 94
Balter, Ann, 26-40, 44, 94, 106

Balter, Ben, 7, 19-25, 26, 27, 28, 39, 44,
    56, 94, 97-98, 177, 185
Balter, Dora, 28
Balter, Gordon, 29, 30, 32, 34, 39
Balter, Harriet, 21, 42
Balter, Iris, 34, 37, 44, 94
Balter, Marguerite, 20-21, 24, 26, 27, 94,
    97-98, 101
Balter, Minnie, 20, 26, 27, 28, 29, 34,
    44, 47, 94, 97, 101
Balter, Nolte, 26
Balter, Norman, 26-40, 44, 94, 102
Balter, Rae, 44, 94
Balter, Ray, 27
Balter, Sam, 28
Balter, Sid, 19-20, 26, 27, 28, 44, 94
Bateman, Ed, 4
Bergman, Celia, 4, 6, 8, 10, 37, 38, 41-
    52, 55, 91, 92, 93, 94, 97, 98, 105
Bergman, Dave, 6, 25, 38, 43, 46, 48-50,
    52, 91, 106, 107, 191
Bernstein, Louis, 51, 95
Berry, Aaron, 127
Berry, Harry, 127
Berry, Jack, 127
Berry, Phil, 127
Beth Sholom Synagogue, 11, 121
Blatt, Maurice, 51, 96
Blatt, Molly, 52, 96

Blatt, Mrs., 51
Blatt, Rowena, 96
Blatt, Sidney, 51, 96
Blatt's Women's Ready-to-Wear, 51-52
Blue Laws, 11
Bodenheim, Betty, 199
Bodenheim, Edwin, 36, 199
Bodenheim, G. A., 36-37, 58, 94, 188
Bodenheim, Roland, 36, 199
Booken, Mr., 95
Booken, Mrs., 52, 95, 101, 102
Brachfield, Benjamin, ix, 141, 160
Brachfield, Charles, 10, 141, 146, 161
Brachfield, Etta, ix, 141, 160
Bramlette, Erskine, 4
Brannon, Jimmy, 55
Brill, Abraham, 124
Brin, Millie, 106
Brin, Phillip, 7, 53-58
Brown, Al, 57

C
Calloway, Cab, 96
Carnagie, Hattie, 173
Carolane's, 95, 170
Castleberry, Mattie, 114, 184
Cockrell, Jim, 55, 56
Cohen, Charlie, 97
Cohen, Henry, 136
Cohen, Ralph, 191
Cohen, Simon, 133
Congregation Beth Sholom, 55, 186
Cook, Dr., 17
Cotton Belt Railroad, 77
Covin, Madeline, 174
Crim, Leggett, 157, 190
Crim Theater, 190
Curley's, 109

D
D&A Oppenheimer, ix
Daiches, Adele, 7-8, 59, 61-65, 67-70
Daiches, Fred, 67
Daiches, Martha, 96
Daiches, Max, 67, 68, 69-70, 110, 115
Daiches, Mrs., 101
Daisy Bradford #3, 4, 143, 144

Davis, Al, 71, 73-80
Davis, Bernard, 40
Davis, Deacon, 175
Davis, Dusty, 175
Davis, E. H., 73
Davis, Jay, 78, 95
Davis, John, 71, 73
Delta Drilling Company, 89, 95, 177
Denowitz, Ben, 170-171
Denowitz, Leona Riff, 170-171
Donsky, Margaret, 94
Donsky, Sam "Honey," 92, 94
Doppelmayer, Daniel, ix, 124
Doppelmayer, Mayer, ix, 124
Dorfman, Elizabeth, 46, 104, 174
Dorfman, Louis, 46
Dorfman Oil Company, 26
Dorfman, Sam, 26, 27, 37, 46, 56, 89,
    95, 104, 115, 174, 177
Dorfman, Sam, Jr., 46
Dorsey, Tommy, 79, 96
Dowd, Jap, 26, 27
Dreyfus & Sons, 137
Duke and Ayers store, 196

E
E. H. and A. Davis clothing store, 73
Eisenberg, Dave, 95
Estes, Carl, 37, 200
Ettelman, Eddie, 185, 190
Ettelman, Louis, 97
Everett Bank building, 36-37

F
F. K. Lathrop No. 1, 4
Faber, Rabbi, 77
Fair Store, 181, 187
Falk, Batty, 85
Falk, Fannie, 85
Falk, Irving, 8, 81, 95
Falk, Louis, 81-82, 85
Falk, Meyer, 85
Feldman, Bessie, 101
Feldman, Henry, 135, 157, 177, 190
Feldman, Larry, 101, 177
Feldman, Phyllis, 106
Feldman, Sam, 177

Feldman, Smoky, 126
Felsenthal, Adolph, 89
Felsenthal, Annette, 100
Felsenthal, Annette Silverberg, 89, 90, 100
Felsenthal, Bernhard, 88, 89
Felsenthal, Daniel, 42, 88, 90, 100
Felsenthal, David, 88-89
Felsenthal, Isaac, 89
Felsenthal, Sherry, 90
Felsenthal, Sonnel, 56, 88, 89, 90, 95, 177
Feltman, Harry, 122
Fensen, Mrs., 52
Finkelstein, Herbert, 57
Finkelstein, Sol, 115, 190
Finlay, Mary Richkie, 195
First National Bank (Longview), 56
Franks, Evelyn, 51, 95
Franks, Manny, 51, 95
Friedlander, Henry, 199
Friedlander, Max, 199
Friedlander, Rosie, 95-96
Friedman, Jack, vii
Frisco Railroad, 42
Frost, Doris, 164
Futoransky, Harry, 51
Futoransky, Iris, 51
Futoransky, Israel, 51
Futoransky, Sophie, 51, 99
Futoransky, Sylvia, 51

G
Gains, Leon, 171
Galoob, Dave, 42, 99-100
Galoob, Debbie, 42, 47, 101
Galoob, Harriet, 101
Galoob, Jack, 96
Galoob, Milton, 8, 27, 29, 34, 35, 40, 43, 44, 47, 51, 91, 92, 93, 96, 97, 100, 101, 109, 154
Galoob, Minnie, *see* Balter, Minnie
Galoob, Rebecca Ammerman Kins, 47, 51, 100
Galoob, Reva, 43, 48, 51, 97, 100
Galoob, Sam, 47
Galoob, Sandi, 47
Galoob, Sarah, 43, 48, 51, 96-97, 100

Gans, DeDe, 10, 103-110
Gans, Leon, 57, 95, 104, 106-107, 109
Gans, May, 104
Gans' Men's Store, 104
Gasway, Bob, 107
Gasway, Johnny, 107
Gelfand, Izzie, 81, 82
Genecov, Alex, 126
Gerson, Joe, 127, 133
Gerstein, Rabbi, 133-134
Gertz, Abe, 134
Gertz, Ben, 134, 185, 190
Gertz, Frances, 133, 190
Gladney, Edna, 90
Glazer, Fritz, 92
Glover-Crim building, 14
Gold, Rose, 46
Gold, Sam, 56
Golden, Bill, 188
Golden, Harry, 115, 126-127, 188, 190
Golden, Joe, 127
Golden, Sam, 190
Goldman, Bill, 157
Goldman, Sam, 11, 55, 115, 126, 156, 185
Gonzaullas, Manuel T. "Lone Wolf," 9, 114, 184
Goodman, Benny, 37, 79, 96
Gordon, Louis, 28-29
Gordon, Sarah, 28
Great Run, The, 99
Great Western Sugar Company, 124

H
Hames, Harry, 37
Hanes, Archie, 27
Hanover, Ike, 127
Harmon Military Hospital, 107, 178
Harris, D. R., 167
Hartman, Madeline, 133
Heidtman, Frank Henry, 195
Heidtman, Nellie Henry, 194
Heidtman, Ralph Malcolm, 195
Heligman, Dr., 156
Henry, Bernard, 95
Hirsch, Joe, 186
Hollywood Café, 54-55

Hopkins, Josephine, 199
hot oil, 75-76, 85-87, 129
Hub Shoe Store, 125
Hunt, H. L., 3, 4, 39, 127
Hurst, Dr., 14, 178
Hurwitz, Ann, 111
Hurwitz, Bill, 120
Hurwitz, Charles, 158-159
Hurwitz, Ethel, 111
Hurwitz, Eva, 113
Hurwitz, Frieda, 111
Hurwitz, Hyman, 9, 11, 39, 110, 111,
    112, 113, 114-115, 117, 118, 120, 134,
    156, 157, 185, 186, 188, 190, 191
Hurwitz, Jean, 119-120, 121
Hurwitz, Lena, 111
Hurwitz, Phillip, 9, 57, 111-115, 117-121
Hurwitz, Sally, 120
Hurwitz, Sam, 57, 111, 112, 113, 115,
    120, 131, 188
Hurwitz, Sidney, 111
Hurwitz, William, 111

I-J
Isenberg, Dave, 126
Jackson, Jake, 127
Jackson, Stella, 142, 161
Jay's Café, 163
Joe Weisman Department Store, 124
Johnny Cace's Seafood Restaurant, 105
Joiner, C. M. "Dad," 1, 3, 143, 193
Joiner, John, 143

K
K. Wolen's store, 51, 57, 95, 162, 196
Karchmer, Madeline, 174
Kariel, Adele, 50-51, 124, 125
Kariel, Louis, 6, 125
Kariel, Louis, Sr., 50, 122-125
Kariel, Maurine, 125
Kariel, Morris, 124
Kariel, Stanley, 125
Katz, Mr., 96
Kennedy, John F., 168
Kerman, Dan, 110, 121, 192
Kins, Celia, 99, 100
Kins, Celia. See Bergman, Celia

Kins, Jack, 41, 45, 48, 50, 91-92, 94, 99,
    100
Kins, Sam, 99, 100
Kins, Sweetie, 94
Krasner, Barney, 6, 126
Krasner, Jene Sobol, 126, 149, 158
Krasner, Sam, 6, 126-127, 149, 158

L
Lamb, Rosa Richkie, 195
Lancer, Marty, 121
Laster, Ed C., 3
Lathrop A-1 well, 197
Laufer, Esther, 131-132, 133
Laufer, Hyman, 9-10, 11-12, 57, 128-
    138, 191
Laufer, Larry, 133
Laufer, Morris, 136
lease hounds, 103, 144
Leibson, Mr., 38, 39
Leibson, Mrs., 51, 101
Levinson, George, 97
Levinson, Ida, 95
Levinson, Izzy, 52, 95
Levinson, Morris, 57
Levitt, Israel, ix
Lewis, Edith, 153
Lewis, Obbie, 153
Liebson, Morris, 51
Lincoln, Abraham, 88, 89
Lindsay, Jerry, 107
Lloyd, Doc, 3
Lone Star Steel Company, 107
Longview Drug Store, 173
Longview Hotel, 105
Longview National Bank, 56
Longview Shoe Store, 171
Lou Della Crim No. 3, 4
Louisiana Iron and Supply Company, 56
Louisiana Pipe and Supply Company,
    95, 177
Lumel, Max, 149
Lumel, Pauline, 149

M
Mantinband, Rabbi Charles, 134
Marcus, Adrian, 123

Marcus, Fannie, 124
Marcus, Marcus, 124
Marcus, Stanley, 178
Margulis, D'voryah, 97
Margulis, Fanye, 97
Margulis, Melvin, 97
Margulis, Morris, 97
Margulis, Rose, 97
Margulis, Sarah, 97
Maritsky, Izadore, 21, 27, 57, 76, 94, 95, 177, 188
Maritsky, Marguerite, *see* Balter, Marguerite
Maritsky Men's Clothing Store, 78
Marwil, Bernard, 142, 161
Marwil, Doris, 164-165, 166, 168
Marwil, Faye, 141
Marwil, Gus, 142, 161
Marwil, Harry, 142, 161
Marwil, Jeannette, 140, 141
Marwil, Leo, 141, 142, 143-144, 145, 161
Marwil, M. H., 139
Marwil, Mike, 4, 140-147
Marwil, Moses, 10, 140, 141-142, 161-163
Marwil, N. L., 140, 141
Marwil, Shirley, 165
Marwil, Stanley, 164, 165
Marwil, Stella, 161-162
Marwilsky, Jeannette Brachfield, 160
Marwilsky, Nathan L., 160
Mattie's Ballroom, 37, 50, 61-62, 78, 79, 83, 96, 97, 105, 109, 114, 163, 184
McCann, Bess, 107
McCarley's Jewelry, 11
McDonald, Martha, 133
Mellon, Harriet Balter, 24
Mellon, Harry, 24
Mellon, Mark, 24
Mellon, Rebecca, 24
Mellon, Stephen, 24
Miller, Mrs., 94, 95
Milstein, Ada, 85, 95, 102
Milstein, Morris, 85, 95
Morgan, C. C., 195-196
Morgan, Crawford, 195

Mundy, Mrs. J. O., 55

N
Neiman-Marcus, 137
New London School, 168
New York Dress Store, 94, 95
Norton and Barbee grocery store, 24

O
Oliver's drugstore, 54
Oppenheimer, Anton, ix

P
Packman, Mr., 51, 62, 95, 170
Palais Royal Ladies' Dress Shop, 62, 170
Parade Refining Company, 4, 127
Pfeffer, Barbara Ann, 63, 65, 66
Pfeffer, Edward, 59, 61
Pfeffer, Sarah Rutstein, 59, 61, 63, 189
Phillips Petroleum, 164
Phillipsborn, Rabbi, 176
Phipps, Jack, 129
Picow, Eddie, 48
Picow, Sarah, 91, 154
Pig Trail Inn, 22, 26
Pilon, Bill, 95
Pinecrest County Club, 106
Pollack, Harry, 149, 152
Pollock, Marie, 150, 152
Pollock, Samuel, 150, 152
Postal Telegraph Company, 92
Presley Elvis, 34-35
Producers Pipe and Supply Company, 95, 177
prorationing, 75, 86, 129

R
R&B Company, 137
Rabicoff, Ana, 153, 159
Rabicoff, Natalie, 159
Rabicoff, S. M. "Mendy," 11, 148
Rabicoff, Sarah Sobol, 100, 148, 149
Rabicoff, Smila, 153, 155, 159
Rabicoff, Smiley, 7, 11, 115, 148, 155
Raisins and Almonds (Rossentier un Mandlin), vii-viii
Reagan, Ronald, 121

"Real Juice Company, The," 92
Rembert National Bank, 172-173
Remer, Vera, 10, 160
Rich Right Café, 178
Richards, Mr., 194
Richkie, Louis, 94, 95, 194, 200
Riff, Carrie Scher, 14, 95, 104, 105, 170-171
Riff, Joe, 7, 51, 62, 63, 95, 107, 170-171
Riff's store, 170-171
Rio Palm Isle, 50, 184
Ritchkie, Louis, 58
Romeo's Restaurant, 106
Roosth, Sam, 126, 157
Rose, Anne, 115, 186
Rose, Bernard, 115, 186
Rudman, Ike, 95, 126
Rudman, Morris, 57
Rudman, Ytis, 95
Rugh, Debbie, 101
Rugh, Peter, 101
Rushing, Dr., 17
Rutstein, Adele, 189

S
Sachse, Mr., 141
Sandler, Harry, 176-177
Sandler Oil Company, 176
Sanger Brothers, 137
Sanger, Shirley, 164
Satchel City, 109
Scher, Abe, 171
Scher, Ilaine, 104
Scher, Nap, 95, 104, 171
Scher, Sally, 95, 104, 171
Scher, Sam, 14
Scher, Thelma, 171
Schnorrers, 79-80
Schulman, Billie, 94
Schulman, Harry, 93-94
Schulman, Jake, 93-94
Schulman, Joe, 93-94
Schulman, Morris, 93-94
Scrinovsky, Ben, 57, 94, 95
Scrinovsky, Bill, 94-95, 127
Seikan, Eva, 63
Seliger, Frank, 51, 96

Seliger, Hilda, 51, 96
Seliger, Lewis, 51, 96
Seliger, Maurice, 51, 96
Selman, Mr., 131
Siegal, Sam, 56, 177
Silverberg, Frank, 89
Silverberg, Marie, 89
Silverberg, Rose, 89, 90
Silverman, Abe, 57, 95, 107
Silverman, Barry, 95
Silverman, D. L., 95
Silverman, David, 95
Silverman, Dora, 95
Silverman, Helen, 95
Silverman, Jack, 95
Silverman, Lana, 95
Silverman, Louis, 95
Sinai Congregation, 88
Sklar and Dorfman, 22
Sklar, Sam, 56
Smith-Connolly Act, 76
Sobol, Charlie, 152, 153, 154
Sobol, Gus, 149
Sobol, Hack, 149
Sobol, Harry, 7, 148, 149
Sobol, Marie, 149
Sobol, Meyer, 149
Sobol, Sarah, 100
Solinger, Leon, 91-92
Solinger, Margaret, 92
Sosland, Abe, 96, 173, 175, 178
Sosland, Dawn, 175, 177
Sosland, Etta Remer, 37-38, 96, 173, 175
Sosland, Helen, 175
Sosland, Jay, 51, 96, 172-178
Sosland, Leonard, 51, 96, 175
Sosland, Marcus, 175
Sosland, Marty, 175
Sosland, Morris, 37, 96, 172-173, 175
Sosland, Sam, 173
Sosland, Shallene, 175
Sosland, Steve, 175
Stag Bar, 92
Statman, Aaron, 137
Statman, Charles, 137, 138
Statman, Irving, 138

Statman, Joe, 137-138
Statman, Louis Craig, 138
Statman, Manya, 137
Statman, Max, 138
Statman, Shayne, 137
Statman, Sherry Michelle, 138
Stein, Harry, 122
Stein, Henry, 122
Steinlein, Nattie, 165
Stern, Dr., 178
Sternberg, Mr., 195
Sterne, Ernestine, ix
Sterne, Jacob, ix
Stidham, Andrea, 137
Stidham, Bryan, 137
Stidham, Joyce Andres, 137
Sugar, Mr., 119

T
T&P Café, 37
Temple Beth Israel, 147
Temple Beth Shalom, 55, 131, 135, 156-157, 169, 176
Temple Beth-El, 115
Temple Emanu-El, 19, 25, 90, 106, 110, 134, 135, 157
Temple Moses Montifiore, 11, 50, 109, 122, 123, 176, 198
Temple Shalom, 65
Temple Zion, 88
Texas Railroad Commission, 75, 86
Texas Rangers, 8-9
Texas Scrap Material Company, 95
Titche-Goettinger, 137
Todd, Katie, 172-173
Toggery, The, 134

Trigger, Charley, 174, 177
Tyler Women's Club, 79

U-W-Y
Unker, Harold, 97
W. A. Green, 137
Waldman, Clara, 8, 179
Waldman, Florence, 119
Waldman, Joseph, 8, 115, 179, 181
Waldman, Nathan, 8, 10-11, 119, 133, 179-192
Walker, Mrs., 46
Waxloch, Lena, 135-136
Weinberg, Herman, 173
Weinberg, Joe, 173
Weinberg Men's Store, 173
Weinstein, Bernie, 51, 57, 95, 107
Weinstein, Ruth, 51, 95
Weinstein, Terrie, 51, 95
Weisman, Carol, 123
Weisman, Fanny, 123
Weisman, Joe, 124
Weisman, Mose, 125
Weisman, Sol, 123
Weldman, Sam, 82, 95, 177
Wessel, Harvey, 18, 134
Whitehurst, Sarah Richkie, 6-7, 93-100, 195
Williams, Mr., 141
Wise, Stephen, 167
Wiseman's Department Store, 173
Wolf, Isaac, ix, 124
Wood, Jack, 128-129
Wood, Leila, 54
Wynne, Angus, 53, 56
Young, Horace, 54

About the Author

Jan Statman is a native of New York City, where she graduated from Hunter College, City University of New York. She arrived in Dallas shortly after graduation and later married and moved to East Texas, where she became fascinated by the land "Behind the Pine Curtain." Along the way she became an artist, art teacher, author, critic, playwright, poet, journalist, and TV interviewer.

Statman is the author of *The Battered Woman's Survival Guide* (Taylor Publishing, Dallas) and *Wet Paint* (Longview Art Museum). She is co-author of *Living with Environmental Illness* (Taylor Publishing). Her feature stories have appeared in such magazines as *Texas Homes, Texas Scene, National Flyer, Republic Scene,* and *American Woman*, and in the *Dallas Morning News*. She wrote the "Final Word" column for the *Dallas Morning News*, "Arts" column for the *Longview News Journal*, and the "Artist's World" column for the *Longview Post*.

Her writing awards include the Exceptional Merit Media Award from the National Women's Political Caucus and Radcliffe College, thirteen Texas Press Women Inc. Annual Communications Contest awards, two National Federation of Press Women's National Communications Contest awards, and two Byline awards in the Corpus Christi, Texas-Wide Writing Competition.

She and her husband Max have three grown children, Charles Barry, Louis Craig, and Sherry Michelle.